NATIONAL BUREAU
OF
ECONOMIC RESEARCH
PUBLICATIONS
IN REPRINT

*See last pages of this volume
for a complete list of titles.*

National Income
A Summary of Findings

Simon Kuznets

ARNO PRESS
A New York Times Company
New York — 1975

Editorial Supervision: Eve Nelson
Reprint Edition 1975 by Arno Press Inc.

Copyright © 1946 by the National Bureau of
   Economic Research, Inc.
Reprinted by permission of the National
   Bureau of Economic Research, Inc.

NATIONAL BUREAU OF ECONOMIC RESEARCH
PUBLICATIONS IN REPRINT
ISBN for complete set: 0-405-07572-3
See last pages of this volume for titles.

Manufactured in the United States of America

———•———

Library of Congress Cataloging in Publication Data

Kuznets, Simon Smith, 1901-
    National income.

    (National Bureau of Economic Research publications
in reprint)
    Reprint of the ed. published by the National Bureau of
Economic Research which was issued as no. 1 of its
Twenty-fifth anniversary series.
    1. National income--United States--Accounting.
I. Title. II. Series. III. Series: National
Bureau of Economic Research. Twenty-fifth anniversary
series, 1.
HC106.K9 1975   339.373   75-19719
ISBN 0-405-07598-7

1

National Income
A Summary of Findings

National Income
A Summary of Findings

Simon Kuznets
University of Pennsylvania

NATIONAL BUREAU OF ECONOMIC RESEARCH, INC.
New York 1946

CONTENTS

TABLES

ACKNOWLEDGMENTS

Throughout the preparation of this report, I have been assisted by Miss Elizabeth Jenks. Comments that served to improve the manuscript were contributed by Morris A. Copeland, Solomon Fabricant, Wesley C. Mitchell, and Ralph A. Young. Miss Martha Anderson edited the report. The effective contribution of these colleagues and friends is gratefully acknowledged.

SIMON KUZNETS

NATIONAL INCOME is the net product of or net return on the economic activity of individuals, business firms, and the social and political institutions that make up a nation. Because product or income yielding activities can be gauged at several stages of the economic process, national income can be measured in various ways, each permitting different groupings of components. At its origin in the productive system, it can be estimated as the sum of returns to the several factors of production—labor, capital, enterprise—each allocated by industrial origin. At this stage, the total can also be obtained by subtracting from the gross value-product of each industry the value of materials, semifabricates, durable capital, and services of other industries consumed in the production process. The corresponding allocation would be that of net income (and of gross value of product) by industrial origin. At the stage of the distribution of money compensation for economic activity, national income is the sum of income receipts of individuals and undistributed net profits of enterprises, the former possibly classified by type (wages, salaries, dividends, etc.), by size among groups of recipients, and by industrial origin, and the latter by industrial affiliation and type of enterprise. Finally, at the stage of use, national product or its monetary equivalent, national income, is the sum of either the flow of goods to consumers and net capital formation, allocated to whatever divisions of these two major categories are significant; or of expenditures and savings of consumers plus outlays of enterprises financed from their undistributed profits, also allocated to divisions of these three major categories.

National income can, therefore, be described in various ways, corresponding to the several stages in the flow-process of economic activity at which it can be measured. However measured, the totals should be identical. Likewise, they can be subdivided into various categories, of which those mentioned above are a few. Indeed, the interest and usefulness of national in-

come estimates lies in their distribution, so that the level of
and changes in the total can be understood and interpreted
in terms of its origin in the industrial system and of types of
ultimate use. As problems in the solution of which national
income estimates may be helpful shift, the emphasis in the
measurement and analysis of national income shifts from one
grouping of components to another.

The task of both subsuming the divers economic activities
within a nation under a single total and distinguishing within
it the major categories raises a host of conceptual and statistical problems. Since World War I these problems have received much attention and the estimates have been extended
and elaborated. In recent years national income, or closely
related totals, has become a tool of public policy, discussed
widely. A jaundiced observer might characterize this interest
and discussion as symptoms of hypochondria, likening them
to the behavior of a man who continually worries about his
pulse, temperature, and blood pressure; and might describe
the more detailed work on national income estimates as an
escape into quantitative minutiae of doubtful relevance to urgent problems of the day. A fairer diagnosis might perhaps
be that, granted the accentuation of economic problems to
whose solution national income estimates can contribute, the
growing interest and understanding are encouraging signs that
social action may be more intelligent; and that the greater
complexity of the statistical structure underlying the estimates
is indispensable, if they are to be sufficiently detailed and reliable to be used in both economic analysis and public policy.

Whatever the reasons, the fact is that during the last twenty-
five years we have learned a great deal about the national
income of this country and its components. In attempting a
brief summary, which must omit many details yet cover the
high spots, we analyze first the structure of national income
during the two decades between the two world wars, then the
longer term changes in it and its components, as revealed by
estimates for the seven decades 1869-1938, consider the fluctuations in it and its components during business cycles, and finally
enumerate some of the problems of use and interpretation.

PART I

Structure, 1919—1938

1 Total and Per Capita

During the two decades 1919-38, national income averaged $66.7 billion per year; somewhat more, $70.5 billion, when expressed in 1929 prices (Table 1). There is a distinct possibility that this total, built up industry by industry from income payments and undistributed net profits of enterprises, is 3 to 5 percent smaller than one derived by other methods.

These figures have little meaning in and of themselves. In recent decades we have learned to associate a specific level of national income in this country with the state of the economy, so that a total of $80 billion in the 1920's and 1930's means relative prosperity and one of $50 billion, acute depression. But even such an interpretation needs to be supplemented with a great deal of other information, if an average level of $70.5 billion in 1929 prices is to have any meaning.

On a per capita basis—of total population, of the gainfully occupied, or of the employed—or in units more akin to us as members of the social system, families and single individuals—the estimates can be grasped better. In 1919-38 national income per capita averaged nearly $600 in 1929 prices; and income distributed, which was almost the same as income produced, averaged somewhat over $2,000 per family (of about 4 members) and nearly $1,500 per single individual per year (Table 1). However, an income of $2,000 in 1929 prices means one thing to a farm family accustomed to a low economic status, and another to an urban family in the upper income brackets. A single national income total, or any measure per population unit derived from it, takes on meaning only when compared with levels characterizing other times or other areas (whether broader or narrower).

3

TABLE 1

National Income and Aggregate Payments, Current and 1929 Prices
Averages for 1919-1938

	CURRENT PRICES (1)	1929 PRICES (2)
National Income		
1 Total ($ billions)	66.7	70.5
2 Per capita ($)	563	591
3 Per gainfully occupied ($)	1,386	1,451
4 Per employed ($)	1,635	1,732
Aggregate Payments incl. Entrepreneurial Savings		
5 Total ($ billions)	66.5	70.7
6 Per capita ($)	560	591
7 Per family type unit		
a Families of 2 or more, per family ($)	1,928	2,050
b Single individuals, per capita ($)	1,378	1,466
c Members of institutional population, per capita ($)	418	445

LINE

1-6 Based on estimates in *National Income and Its Composition* (National Bureau of Economic Research, 1941), particularly Vol. One, Tables 1, 5, and 8. Minor revisions were made in the population series and in the adjustment of the income totals to 1929 prices. Other minor revisions could have been made in the estimates of the gainfully occupied and of the employed, yielding slightly higher averages in lines 3 and 4. But they were not deemed sufficiently important for the purpose at hand.

In this table, and throughout this report, 'employed' includes employed wage earners and salaried workers (with those employed part-time converted, wherever possible, to full-time equivalent units) and all entrepreneurs, without any allowance for their unemployment or part-time engagement.

7 Based upon the proportional division of total population and aggregate income for 1935-36 between families, single individuals, and the institutional population in *Consumer Incomes in the United States* (National Resources Committee, Washington, D. C., 1938), Table 1, p. 4. The proportions were applied to the average population and average aggregate payments for 1919-38. The average number of families (3.9444 persons per family) was estimated to be 27.426 million; of single individuals, 9.313 million; of members of the institutional population, 1.910 million.

Such comparisons cannot be made in detail here. All we can say is that national income per capita, per gainfully occupied, per employed, or per consuming unit in the United States, with allowances for differences in purchasing power of the monetary units, was not only one of the highest in the world, indeed the highest among the major countries,[1] but also the highest

[1] For evidence, see Colin Clark, *Conditions of Economic Progress* (Macmillan, 1940), particularly Chapter II. For many countries Mr. Clark's estimates are obviously subject to a wide margin of error, some of which can already be corrected. But the rough nature of the estimates does not affect the conclusion that, judged by its national income per capita in the 1920's and the 1930's, the United States was at

in the history of this country before this war, although the two decades include the severest cyclical depression on record (Table 10).

How was this high per capita income produced and used? The answer will perhaps be typical of other industrially advanced, large countries that are also in the upper part of the pyramid of the distribution of world income by the size of the country's per capita.

2 Distribution by Industrial Origin

The industrial classification in Table 2 is not the most detailed available for the period: many more industrial branches are distinguished in *National Income and Its Composition* (National Bureau of Economic Research, 1941; see particularly Ch. 5, pp. 161-214). But the chief lines of the industrial structure of national income stand out.

First, the share of the commodity producing industries, 38 percent, is smaller than that of the service industries—governmental, professional, personal, etc.—which is 42 percent; commodity transporting and distributing account for 20 percent. Such a primary industry as agriculture accounts for less than one-tenth. The distribution of the part of national income that goes as compensation to employees and entrepreneurs, i.e., largely as return for personal effort, is quite similar to that of national income; a somewhat larger share goes to commodity production and to commodity transportation and distribution and a somewhat smaller to the service industries.

The industrial structure of the working force is quite different. Almost a half is engaged in commodity producing industries, just over one-fifth in agriculture, and less than a third in the service industries.

These contrasts indicate big differences among industries in income per member of the working population (Table 2, col.

---

the top of the pyramid, the wide base of which was made up of the huge populous countries of Asia and Africa (British India, China, and the like) whose national income per capita was not more, and perhaps less, than one-tenth that of this country.

TABLE 2

National Income, Service Income (both in Current Prices), and Aggregate Employment, Percentage Distribution by Industry
(based on averages of percentages for 1919-38)

	PERCENTAGE SHARES IN			RATIO OF INCOME PER WORKER IN INDUSTRY TO INCOME PER WORKER IN COUNTRY	
	National Income	Service Income	Aggregate Employment	Service Income (2)÷(3)	Total Income (1)÷(3)
	(1)	(2)	(3)	(4)	(5)
PART A BY MAJOR INDUSTRIAL DIVISIONS					
1 Agriculture	9.5	10.9	20.6	0.5	0.5
2 Mining	2.1	2.5	2.4	1.0	0.9
3 Manufacturing	20.7	22.2	21.7	1.0	1.0
4 Construction	3.6	4.5	3.4	1.3	1.0
5 Transp. & other public utilities	9.9	8.6	7.0	1.2	1.4
6 Trade	13.6	16.0	14.2	1.1	1.0
7 Finance & real estate	11.9	4.3	3.0	1.4	4.0
8 Service	12.7	15.6	15.3	1.0	0.8
9 Government	12.0	11.0	7.8	1.4	1.5
10 Miscellaneous	3.9	4.5	4.5	1.0	0.9
PART B BY PRODUCTIVE FUNCTION					
11 Commodity production	37.6	40.9	48.8	0.8	0.8
a Primary	9.5	10.9	20.6	0.5	0.5
b Secondary	28.2	30.0	28.2	1.1	1.0
12 Tertiary	62.3	59.2	51.2	1.2	1.2
a Commod. transp. & distribution	19.9	22.1	19.0	1.2	1.0
b Services	42.4	37.1	32.2	1.2	1.3
PART C BY PREDOMINANT TYPE OF ORGANIZATION					
13 Large prop. of indiv. firms	52.2	52.6	59.2	0.9	0.9
14 Private corp.	22.8	24.7	24.1	1.0	0.9
15 Semi-public corp.	12.9	11.8	8.9	1.3	1.4
16 Public	12.0	11.0	7.8	1.4	1.5

For definition of 'aggregate employment' see note to Table 1.

COLUMN
1 Averages of annual estimates in *National Income and Its Composition*, Vol. One, Table 59.
2 Averages of annual estimates in *ibid.*, Table 67.
3 Averages of annual estimates in *ibid.*, Table 69.

Industrial classification of lines 11-16:
LINE
11a Agriculture
11b Mining, manufacturing, construction, electric light and power, manufactured gas
12a Steam railroads, Pullman, and express, water transportation, pipe lines, trade
12b Street railways, telephone, telegraph, finance and real estate, service, government, miscellaneous
13   Agriculture, construction, trade, real estate, service, miscellaneous
14   Mining, manufacturing
15   Transportation and other public utilities, banking, insurance
16   Government

5). In agriculture income per employed is half that in all industries combined; and in transportation and other public utilities, finance, and government, well above the countrywide average. When industries are classified by their productive function, income per employed is below the countrywide average in primary commodity production; at the average in secondary commodity production and in commodity transportation and distribution; and well above the average in the service industries.

Income per employed reflects not only the productivity assignable to the worker personally and measured by his compensation but also the amount of capital invested and the relative weight of property income originating in the industry. It is the large share of the latter that explains the very high ratio for finance and real estate and the relatively low ratio for the service industry in column 5. A better approximation to inter-industry differences in the income productivity of the working force proper is provided if we exclude property income (col. 4). Agriculture is still characterized by relatively low income per employed; in construction, transportation and other public utilities, finance and real estate, and government, income per employed is relatively high. The somewhat surprising showing for the service industry, for which we would expect a ratio above 1.0, is due to the offsetting of the high levels for professional service by the low levels for domestic service. In the distribution by type of productive function, differences in service income per employed roughly parallel those in total income per employed (col. 5).

The differences among industries in income per employed are obviously due to many factors. Those that come to mind most readily are differences in the supply of personal capital (embodied in skill and training); in the bargaining power of the several industries in procuring for their workers the greatest return for their services; in the different pricing of the same or comparable products and services as between country and city, small town and metropolis; in the cost of living associated with conditions of life imposed upon workers by their affiliation with one industry or another. While many other factors may be at play, a large part of inter-industry differences in service income per worker is ascribable to inter-industry disparities in costs, either past (represented by education and training) or present (represented by higher living costs). In other words, a shift in the working force from agriculture to professional service will, other conditions being equal, serve to raise income per capita and national income at large, but the price will be greater diversion of income to training; moreover, a greater share will go to cover additional expenses of living associated with the urban conditions under which most professional practice is pursued.

When the minor industrial divisions are grouped by the prevailing type of firm, a relatively large share of national income is accounted for by industries dominated by individual firms and a moderate share by those dominated by corporations, even including the public utilities, which the extent of government control makes semipublic (Table 2, lines 13-16). Whether in national income, service income, or aggregate employment, the share of industries dominated by individual firms is well over one-half, and that of corporations about one-third. While the distribution is crude and the share of individual firms possibly exaggerated, even a finer allocation would attribute to individual firms at least as large a share of national income and probably a larger share of the working force than to corporations. The impression that the economic scene is dominated by the latter is possibly due to their greater share of the commodity capital of the industrial system, and even more, to the concentration of activity under the auspices of a few large units.

Total and service income per employed rise steadily as we pass from the group with a large proportion of individual firms to the industries dominated by private corporations, to those in which corporations are subject to more government regulation, and finally to the public sector. This association between degree of departure from free and decentralized operations by a large number of individual firms and the relative level of income per worker may be fortuitous or due to causes other than the extent and character of the regulation.

But it may well be that the more regulated and monopolistic an industry, the greater the possibility of a pre-selection of its working force, to assure higher per worker productivity and to justify the higher income; or of a higher per capita return because of an advantageous position in the markets of the economy.

3 Distribution by Type

The estimates show that of national income produced during the two decades, more than 100 percent, on the average, was distributed in the form of income payments (Table 3), partly because we averaged percentages, partly because of the severe depression from 1929 to 1932. But even in the cyclically prosperous year 1929 the share of national income retained as undistributed net profits by corporations and savings by governments was only 4 percent; and thus the amount *not* distributed to recipients in the form of income payments ordinarily constitutes merely a minor fraction of national income.

Roughly four-fifths is service income, i.e., returns largely for personal effort; one-fifth property income, i.e., returns on invested capital. A fine line cannot be drawn between returns for personal effort and on capital; e.g., entrepreneurial income presumably includes some compensation for the entrepreneur's equity in his business (i.e., his own capital invested in it) and some return to the factor of enterprise similar to that of undistributed net profits of corporations. But since most entrepreneurs are in farming, retail trade, and the service industry, it is fair to assume that by far the major proportion of their total income is compensation for their personal services, similar in character to payments to a wage earner or salaried employee. It can therefore be concluded that on the average, compensation for personal effort accounts for at least three-fourths of national income, and returns on property and enterprise for less than one-fourth.

The relative weight of service and property income varies from industry to industry and with the amount of capital invested in proportion to the direct services of employees and

TABLE 3

Percentage Distribution by Type of Income, National Income and
Net Income Originating (both in Current Prices) in
Broad Industrial Divisions by Predominant Type of Organization
(based on averages of percentages for 1919-38)

	ALL INDUSTRIES (NATIONAL INCOME)	BROAD INDUSTRIAL DIVISIONS BY PREDOMINANT TYPE OF ORGANIZATION (NET INCOME ORIGINATING)				
		LARGE PROPORTION OF INDIVIDUAL FIRMS		PRIVATE CORP.	SEMI-PUBLIC CORP.	PUBLIC
		Incl. Rent	Excl. Rent			
	(1)	(2)	(3)	(4)	(5)	(6)
1 Employee compensation	64.1	50.2	56.2	87.2	71.4	74.3
2 Entrep. net income	17.5	31.8	35.7	2.4	2.5	0.0
3 Service income (1–2)	81.6	82.0	91.9	89.6	73.8	74.3
4 Dividends	6.2	2.5	2.8	13.6	14.3	0.0
5 Interest	7.4	6.8	7.6	1.5	10.7	18.2
6 Rent	5.7	10.8	...	0.0	0.0	0.0
7 Property income incl. rent (4–6)	19.3	20.1	10.4	15.1	25.0	18.2
8 Corp. & gov. net savings	—0.9	—2.1	—2.3	—4.7	1.2	7.5

Based on annual data underlying Table 23, *National Income and Its Composition,* Vol. One.

entrepreneurs. If rent is excluded as not susceptible of a proper industrial allocation with the present data, the share of service income is highest in the industries dominated by individual firms—averaging 92 percent; the amount of capital invested in proportion to the direct services of employees and entrepreneurs is small; and part of the returns on capital are included under entrepreneurial net income. Also, the share of entrepreneurial net income is relatively high, much higher than in the other major industrial categories or in national income.

In the group dominated by private corporations, the share of service income is lower and that of property income higher. The peculiarities of these industries (mining and manufacturing) also account for the fact that in property income dividends are so much more important than interest.

The share of property income is highest in the public utilities group—indicating the large weight of capital invested in proportion to labor. Although less than that of dividends, the share of interest is substantial, reflecting the importance of bonds as a method of providing long term capital for steam railroads and related older public utilities.

Finally, in government of course there is neither entrepreneurial net income nor dividends. The somewhat unexpectedly large share of governmental savings is due largely to the use of a sizable proportion of current revenues in public works productive of additions to durable capital owned by the government. While for other industries the percentage of net savings for the period was negative, it was positive for both public utilities and government. This, however, is an idiosyncrasy of this period rather than a long standing characteristic of the structure of national income in this country.

The distribution of national income by type serves as a link between the industrial structure and the distribution of income payments by size. Differences in industrial structure between periods or countries spell differences in the distribution by type: the greater the weight of agriculture and of industries similarly dominated by individual firms, the larger the share of entrepreneurial income. The larger the share of industries that must employ huge amounts of direct services and cannot employ proportionate amounts of invested capital (e.g., agriculture, trade, the service industry, mining, construction, and even some branches of manufacturing), the larger the share of service income and the smaller the share of property income.

Being thus determined, at least in large degree, by the industrial structure of the country's productive system, the distribution of national income by type in turn affects the distribution of income payments by size. Employee compensation gives rise to a different size distribution than dividends or interest. Consequently, varying shares of wages, salaries, entrepreneurial income, dividends, interest, rent, etc. ordinarily make for different distributions of income payments by size among recipients. Other conditions being the same, a larger proportion of service income gives incomes in the lower brackets a greater weight in the total distribution and incomes in the higher brackets a smaller.

4 Distribution by Size

On the size distribution of income payments no continuous annual data are available. The only body of information provided annually during the two decades 1919-38 are summaries of federal income tax returns by individuals, which cover a small percentage of all income recipients and a relatively low proportion of the country's total population.

By comparing the information from federal returns with total income payments we can ascertain for each year the fraction received by persons in the higher brackets. The comparison requires several detailed technical adjustments, designed to correct for the use in the federal income tax data of a net income concept that differs in several important respects from individuals' incomes defined as shares in national income. Further adjustments are needed to ascertain the proportion that the number of persons represented on income tax returns constitutes of the total population. These various adjustments and calculations cannot be explained in detail here. In general, the persons represented on tax returns are grouped by their total income from the highest to the lowest each year. In the distribution of the 'income tax population' and its total income, thus cumulated from the top incomes downward, lines are interpolated segregating the top 1, 2, 3, 4, etc. percents of total population, yielding the percentages of total income payments received by these upper income groups. The lowest dividing line that can be drawn from the income tax data year-in-year-out is the 5 percent line.

The upper 1 percent of the population received, on the average, 14 percent of total income payments, and about 1 percent less if we allow for the part of tax payments that can be measured annually, viz., federal income taxes (omitting such taxes from both the income receipts of the upper 1 percent of the population and those of the total population) (Table 4). The upper 5 percent of the population received, on the average, over a quarter of total income payments, and again about 1 percent less, if we deduct federal income taxes from all income payments. Because of difficulty in passing from the published distributions of tax returns by size of net income (tax definition) per return to the desired distribution by size of economic income per person, and because of possible under-reporting on tax returns, the percentages in Table 4 are

TABLE 4

Percentage Shares of Total Income Payments (Current Prices)
Received by Upper and Lower Income Groups
(based on averages of percentages for 1919-38)

	INCOME GROUPS OF TOTAL POPULATION			
	Upper 1% (1)	Upper 5% (2)	Lower 95% (3)	Total (4)
1 % share of total income payments, adj. for marital status				
a Excl. fed. income taxes	12.8	25.4	74.6	100.0
b Incl. fed. income taxes	13.7	26.3	73.7	100.0
2 % shares of various types of payment, unadj. for marital status & incl. fed. income taxes				
a Employee compensation	6.5	16.9	83.1	100.0
b Entrep. net income	13.7	26.9	73.1	100.0
c Service income	8.1	19.1	80.9	100.0
d Dividends	69.7	82.4	17.6	100.0
e Interest	25.7	38.8	61.2	100.0
f Rent	17.9	38.3	61.7	100.0
g Property income incl. rent	40.1	54.2	45.8	100.0
h Total income payments	13.1	24.7	75.3	100.0
3 % distribution by type of total income received, unadj. for marital status & incl. fed. income taxes				
a Employee compensation	33.0	45.4	72.8	66.0
b Entrep. net income	19.0	19.9	17.6	18.2
c Service income	51.9	65.3	90.4	84.2
d Dividends	30.9	19.5	1.4	5.9
e Interest	13.2	10.6	5.7	6.9
f Rent	3.9	4.5	2.5	3.0
g Property income incl. rent	48.1	34.7	9.6	15.8
h Total income	100.0	100.0	100.0	100.0

Based on a comparison of data on individuals' federal income tax returns with estimates of income payments. The detailed analysis is now being prepared for a monograph, *Some Aspects of the Distribution of Income by Size.* An earlier analysis along these lines was made by Morris A. Copeland in *Recent Economic Changes,* II, 833-7.

The percentage distribution in col. 4, lines 3a-g, differs from that in Table 3, col. 1, because the total distributed here differs from that in Table 3 in that it includes entrepreneurial savings adjusted for gains and losses on the sale of assets rather than unadjusted, and excludes: (a) imputed rent on owner-occupied residences; (b) property income of life insurance companies; (c) savings of corporations and of governments.

probably too low. But the resulting underestimate in the shares of upper income groups, according to various tests, does not exceed one-tenth. The average share of the upper 1 percent is thus probably closer to 15 percent than to 14 (line 1b); and of the upper 5 percent, to 29 than to 26 percent.

While the upper 1 percent of the population received, on the average, one-seventh of total income payments, its shares in the countrywide totals of the several types of income differed widely. On the basis of the only variant for which analysis by type of income is possible (the estimate not adjusted for differences in number of persons per return between marital status groups or for exclusion of federal income taxes), the average share of the upper 1 percent in total wages and salaries was below 7 percent; but as high as 70 percent in total dividends. This does *not* mean that of all wages and salaries about one-fourteenth and of dividends about seven-tenths were distributed in such big lumps as in themselves to place the recipient and his dependents in the upper 1 percent of the population: an income may consist of a receipt from a single source or of receipts from sources of various types. Multi-type income receipts are much more common in the upper than in the lower brackets. Lines 2a-g in Table 4 show, then, not differences in the inequality of distribution by size of wages, dividends, etc., but merely differences among wages and salaries, dividends, etc. in their distribution between the various population groups, classified by size of *total* income per person.

As a result of the differences shown in lines 2a through 2g, incomes of the upper groups are much more heavily weighted by dividends and other income from property than those of the lower. Indeed, on the average, dividends, interest, and rents combined account for almost half of the incomes of the upper 1 percent of population; and for over one-third of the incomes of the upper 5 percent (Table 4, lines 3a-g). For the lower 95 percent of the population, they constitute less than one-tenth, for the entire population, about one-sixth.

Table 4 tells nothing about the characteristics of the income distribution among the masses below the upper 5 percent line. Comprehensive information on the distribution of income by size in this country is available only for 1935-36. Though the data are for only one year and are derived from a small sample, the general conclusions they suggest are likely to be fairly typical of other years.

In the distribution of income among families (excluding the much smaller groups of single individuals and the institutional population), inequality is marked even below the high upper level. For example, the lowest tenth of families received only 2 percent of total income payments; the ninth tenth, 15 percent, or over 7 times as much.[2]

Some of the factors making for such inequality and the general characteristics of the family income distribution are suggested in Table 5. Nonrelief families can be grouped into a few occupational-industry classes, and some measures of skewness and inequality are given or can be calculated. The various groups differ greatly in the average level of income per family, whether measured by median or arithmetic mean: farm families receive the lowest incomes (if we exclude relief families and the heterogeneous category, 'other'); families whose income was mainly from independent professional practice the highest. The arithmetic mean income is consistently larger than the median, indicating that all these family income distributions are skewed in the direction of the larger incomes, appreciably so for most groups. This positive skewness is least among the wage earning and clerical groups; greatest among the business, independent professional, and 'other' families. As measured by the proportion of families whose incomes are 25 or 50 percent below or above the median income, there is least inequality within clerical, salaried professional, salaried business, and wage earning (excluding relief) families; and most within groups of independent entrepreneurs—farming, business, professional—and 'other', particularly independent professional and 'other'.[3]

These conclusions accord fully with expectations: the higher

---

[2]*Consumer Incomes in the United States* (National Resources Committee, Washington, D. C., 1938), Table 6B, p. 96.

[3]The proportions of families with incomes 25 or 50 percent above or below the median income do no reflect the effect upon inequality of very low or very high incomes. But they do approximate the degree to which families are bunched about the median income, or scattered far from it.

These conclusions are confirmed by the Lorenz curves in Milton Friedman and Simon Kuznets, *Income from Independent Professional Practice* (National Bureau of Economic Research, 1945), Ch. 3, Charts 2 and 3.

TABLE 5

Some Aspects of the Distribution of Family Income by Size
Total and Groups by Occupational and Employment Status, 1935-1936

GROUPS	NO. OF FAMILIES (mill.)	MEDIAN INCOME ($)	ARITHMETIC MEAN INCOME ($)	RATIO OF MEAN TO MEDIAN	% OF FAMILIES WITHIN 75-125% of Median	50-150% of Median
	(1)	(2)	(3)	(4)	(5)	(6)
1 All families	29.4	1,160	1,622	1.40	28.6	53.9
2 Relief families	4.5	685	740	1.08	29.5	59.3
3 Nonrelief familes	24.9	1,285	1,781	1.39	29.7	56.5
Groups under 3						
4 Farming	6.2	965	1,259	1.30	29.1	56.2
5 Wage earning						
a Nonrelief	9.5	1,175	1,289	1.10	35.1	63.1
b Incl. relief (5a + 2)	14.0	987	1,130	1.14	32.8	57.7
6 Clerical	3.6	1,710	1,901	1.11	38.9	70.0
7 Salaried business	1.1	2,485	4,212	1.69	35.4	64.7
8 Independent business	2.4	1,515	2,547	1.68	28.9	55.8
9 Salaried professional	0.99	2,100	3,087	1.47	37.6	65.1
10 Independent professional	0.34	3,540	6,734	1.90	23.1	46.1
11 'Other'	0.85	745	1,696	2.28	22.0	43.0

Taken or calculated from various tables in *Consumer Incomes in the United States*. Families alone are covered in the above estimates; single individuals and the institutional population are excluded. Relief families include all families receiving any direct or work relief, however little, at any time during the year.

Families are classified by the occupation from which largest family earnings were derived, rather than by the occupation of the principal earner. 'Farming' families include families living on farms in rural areas only. 'Other' families include families with no income from earnings during the year, and village and urban families with major earnings from farming.

levels of average income in the pursuits that require either greater investment in training and education (professional and salaried business) or in equity capital (independent business) or in urban cost of living (all urban as compared with farm); the greater skewness to the right in occupations that by their nature admit of qualitative differentiation to very high levels of particular excellence or success (such as business and independent professional); the greater inequality in pursuits where the qualitative range can be very wide.

Any interpretation in terms of welfare must be qualified stringently. Being for only one year, the data reflect transient influences which temporarily depress some incomes and temporarily raise others. Magnified as it is by these transient influences, the range of inequality cannot be interpreted as a range of differences in income *status;* i.e., income position during, say, a quinquennium or decade. Furthermore, differences in income cannot be interpreted as differences in welfare, for the cost of living varies widely in different parts of the country and for different groups of the population; i.e., identical or comparable bundles of goods do not cost the same everywhere. The differences are positively associated with the size of income, i.e., living costs are usually higher the larger the monetary income. So far as this is true, welfare does not parallel monetary income. On the other hand, if income falls below a certain minimum level for any substantial period, the negative effect on welfare is much greater than is reflected by a sheer numerical difference between the dollar level of that income and of another above the minimum welfare line. So far as the distribution includes any large groups whose income is below the minimum, welfare differences are greater than would be suggested by numerical comparisons of dollar income alone.

Distributions of money income by size among recipients are a basic datum in calculating taxation bases or propensities to consume and to save. But in evaluating the adequacy of the income structure from the welfare viewpoint they must be used together with information on size of income for a fairly long period, with data on the costs of living at various levels of want satisfaction and welfare which would reflect the variety of living and cost patterns among groups in different parts of the country. The present state of our information in this vast and still relatively unexplored field is such that we cannot do more than indicate a few characteristics of the distribution of income by size and the difficulty of interpreting them in terms of welfare.

5　*Distribution by Type of Use*

Net product, whose monetary equivalent we call national income, goes into various channels. Part of it flows to ultimate consumers to satisfy wants and to provide the material basis for survival, reproduction, and growth. Another part is added to the stock of capital goods within the country, or to claims against foreign countries. National income, by definition, is divided between the flow of goods to ultimate consumers and net capital formation, i.e., net addition to the stock of goods outside households and to claims against foreign countries.

It can be allocated also among subcategories of use. In the flow of goods to consumers we distinguish major groups by length of average life in the consumption process: (1) perishable commodities (lasting less than six months—food, drugs, fuel, paper products, etc.) ; (2) semidurable (lasting from six months to three years—clothing and shoes, tires, the lighter type of housefurnishings, etc.) ; (3) durable (lasting more than three years—passenger cars, furniture, etc.) ; (4) services not embodied in new commodities—ranging from services of commodities (such as residences and transportation facilities), services applied to commodities already in the hands of ultimate consumers (for repair and maintenance), to services rendered directly to ultimate consumers by individuals (professional practitioners, domestic servants, governments). The importance of the classification lies in the relation between the average durability of a good and the responsiveness of the demand for it to cyclical and other short term influences. New residential units, while logically classifiable under the flow of goods to ultimate consumers, are put under net capital formation, the purchase being treated as an investment rather than as a consumer expenditure.

Net capital formation too can be allocated—to construction (of various descriptions, by type of use), the flow of producers' equipment, net addition to inventories, and net changes in claims against foreign countries. The total is net in that from the annual gross value of construction and producer durable equipment turned out during the year we deduct the value of construction and durable equipment consumed in the production process.

During the two decades 1919-38 the flow of goods to consumers accounted for well over 90 percent of national income, leaving only 6-7 percent for net capital formation (Table 6). The relative distribution between the two changes materially with the business cycle, and the apportionment for 1919-38 may be unduly affected, as a measure of the disposition char-

TABLE 6

National Income, Percentage Distribution by Type of Use
(based on average values for 1919-38)

	% DISTRIBUTION OF NATIONAL INCOME		% DISTRIBUTION OF COMPONENTS	
	Current Prices (1)	1929 Prices (2)	Current Prices (3)	1929 Prices (4)
Flow of Goods to Consumers				
1 Perishable	35.8	37.8	38.4	40.1
2 Semidurable	14.5	13.6	15.6	14.4
3 Durable	9.2	9.0	9.9	9.5
4 Services	33.6	34.0	36.1	36.1
5 Total	93.2	94.3	100.0	100.0
Net Capital Formation				
6 Producer durable	1.4	1.3	21.0	23.6
7 Construction	3.1	2.8	46.0	49.8
8 Net addition to inventories	1.4	0.8	20.2	14.1
9 Net changes in claims against foreign countries	0.9	0.7	12.9	12.6
10 Total	6.8	5.7	100.0	100.0
11 National income (5 + 10)	100.0	100.0		

Based on estimates in *National Product since 1869* (National Bureau of Economic Research, 1946), Tables II 8, 15, and 16.

acteristic of recent decades, by the severe contraction of 1929-32. But the general conclusion, viz., that of the current net product the overwhelming share, about nine-tenths, flows to ultimate consumers, and only a minor share remains for addition to capital stock, may be accepted as typical of the disposition of national income in this country.[4]

Of the total flow of goods to ultimate consumers, about 40 percent is accounted for by perishable commodities and an almost equally large share by services. These two categories together account also for over 70 percent of national income (in 1929 prices). As both include goods that disappear in the very process of consumption, one is left with the impression that of the current net product of economic activity a very large

[4]Calculations based upon the ratio of individuals' monetary savings to their income receipts are likely to exaggerate the ratio of net capital formation to national income for several reasons. Part of individuals' monetary savings is a fund laid aside for depreciation on owner-occupied residences (usually treated as savings by individuals but not representing real net investment). Many calculations include gains and losses on capital assets under income, and the savings of those who have realized capital gains are not offset by the hidden dissavings of the individuals who have financed these capital gains by purchasing the assets.

proportion vanishes without leaving a trace in the stock of goods. Correlatively, one is inclined to infer the urgent need of maintaining and increasing national income as a means of satisfying the current wants of ultimate consumers.

But the small share of net capital formation and of the *physically* durable components of the flow of goods to consumers should not be interpreted to mean that current consumption of perishable goods does not contribute to the future capacity of the economy. Indeed, one may argue that its effect is at least as great as that of additions to commodity capital in either business enterprises or households. For a country's greatest capital asset is its people, with their skill, experience, and drive toward useful economic activity. To keep these at a high level the flow of perishable commodities and of services (as well as the flow of goods to consumers in general) is crucial. The effects of a high standard of living, assured by an adequate flow of perishable and other commodities, and of the skills generated by such a 'perishable' service as education, are, of course, immense. Hence, even if we forget that, after all, national income is for the consumer and not the consumer for national income; even if we look upon national income chiefly as a means to accumulate capital and augment the country's future productive capacity, substantial portions of the flow of goods to consumers, whether in the perishable or the more durable categories, should be treated as comparable in importance to net capital formation.

By using data on commodity flow in conjunction with those on savings of enterprises and of individuals and with those on assets of various owner-categories, we can distinguish the sources of net capital formation and the broad groups of industries in which net construction and net additions to producers' equipment took place (Table 7).

Savings embodied in net capital formation are accumulated mainly by individuals. Undistributed corporate profits were on the average negative in 1919-38; and even in the prosperous decade 1919-28 constituted little more than a tenth of the average volume of net capital formation. Similarly, government savings, while substantial, were minor compared with the savings of individuals. The latter amounted to over 95 percent of net capital formation over the full period; almost 70 percent even in the prosperous decade 1919-28.

The sample data for 1935-36 suggest that individuals' savings, which are so large relatively to the country's average

TABLE 7

Sources and Destination of Net Capital Formation

	BILLIONS OF DOLLARS (1)	PERCENTAGE SHARES (2)
A Net Capital Formation by Type of Savings		
Averages for 1919-38, Current Prices		
1 Total	4.6	100.0
2 Corporate savings	—0.4	—9.9
3 Government savings	0.7	14.5
4 Individuals' savings, incl. entrep. savings [1 — (2 + 3)]	4.3	95.4
Averages for 1919-28, Current Prices		
5 Total	7.9	100.0
6 Corporate savings	1.0	13.0
7 Government savings	1.4	17.4
8 Individuals' savings, incl. entrep. savings [5 — (6 + 7)]	5.5	69.6

	% OF NUMBER		
B Sources of Individuals' Savings by Income Groups (based on data for 1935-36)			
9 Lower third of families & single individuals	33.3	—1.21	—20.2
10 Middle third of families & single individuals	33.3	—0.25	—4.2
11 Upper third of families & single individuals	33.4	7.44	124.4
a $1,450– 2,000	15.2	0.46	7.7
b 2,000– 3,000	11.2	1.07	17.9
c 3,000– 5,000	4.6	1.18	19.6
d 5,000–15,000	1.9	1.90	31.8
e 15,000 & over	0.5	2.83	47.4
12 Total	100.0	5.98	100.0

C Industrial Distribution of Increase in Value of Real Estate Improvements & Equipment, 1929 Prices (Jan. 1, 1919 — Jan. 1, 1939)		
13 Private industry, excl. public utilities	5.0	12.5
14 Public utilities	14.9	37.2
15 Residential	6.8	16.9
16 Total private (13-15)	26.7	66.6
17 Tax exempt	13.4	33.4
18 Total of above	40.2	100.0

LINE   COLUMN 1

1 & 5 From *National Product since 1869*, Table II 15.

2, 3, Averages of annual estimates in *National Income and Its Composition*, 6, & 7 Vol. One, Table 39.

9-12 *Consumer Expenditures in the United States* (National Resources Committee, Washington, D. C., 1939), Table 1 A, p. 77.

13-18 *National Product since 1869*, Table IV 13, Part B.

COLUMN 2

Based on absolute values in col. 1.

real net investment, come primarily from the upper income groups. The savings of families and single individuals with incomes of $5,000 and over, who accounted for one-fortieth of total income receiving units, constituted almost eight-tenths of the total saved by individuals. Even if we assume that peculiarities of the sample exaggerate the relative importance of the upper income groups in total savings, the dominance of the relatively few high income recipients can hardly be gainsaid.

The largest part of net capital formation—construction and producers' equipment—can alone be classified by broad channels of destination, although the data do not admit of an accurate distribution by sufficiently narrow categories of users (Table 7, lines 13-18). In 1919-38 private industries—excluding public utilities—received one-eighth of net additions to construction and equipment. Public utilities, as always, accounted for a substantial share—well over one-third. All private, including residential, constituted two-thirds of the total, leaving one-third for all tax exempt—government and other public—largely the former. As will be seen in Part II, the distribution is not typical of the longer past in that too large a share is assigned to tax exempt and too small a share to private industries excluding public utilities—a reflection of the severe depression of the 1930's.

At this point, our tracing of the economic process of circulation as reflected in national income and its components—from its origin in the various industries, through its distribution by type and size, to the various categories of use of both income flow and national product—is completed. Many of the characteristics noted are interconnected; e.g., the high level of national income per capita, the moderate share of agriculture and the relatively large share of service industries, the type of organization, the relatively large share of employee compensation and the small share of entrepreneurial income, the skewness and rather marked inequality of the distribution by size, the relatively large share of the flow of goods to consumers and the correspondingly small share of net capital formation, and finally the dominance of savings by those of individuals in the upper income brackets. They are the characteristics of a highly developed industrial, largely urban economy, with a relatively democratic organization of society and freedom of enterprise.

In a country as large as this, with room for wide differences among regions, with contrasts between huge metropolitan centers and vast rural areas, there must be substantial regional and community-size differences in the level of income per capita and in the various characteristics of income composition. We now summarize briefly this aspect of the structure of national income.

6 *Regional and Community-size Differences*

Income per capita differs markedly from state to state, ranging from well below one-half of the countrywide average in Mississippi to over one and one-half times in New York (Table 8). States are, to some extent, artificial units; and from the data underlying the averages, income per capita cannot be determined precisely. Yet obviously dollar levels of per capita income differ so widely from one part of the country to another that the countrywide average is not representative. If income per capita in the country as a whole doubled from about 1880 to the 1920's and 1930's we might say that the states whose per capita income was 40 or 50 percent below the countrywide average in the 1920's were at the 1880 stage; whereas those whose per capita income was as much as 50 percent above the average were at the 1960 or 1970 stage.[5]

In general, a high level of income per capita is associated with a high proportion of income from industries other than agriculture; and a low level with a dominant share of agriculture in the state's productive system; the coefficient of rank correlation between columns 2 and 1 is 0.74, high enough to be significant. In view of the lower level of income per worker in agriculture than in other industries, discussed in Section 2.

[5]The analogy is not quite fair since it disregards the accessibility to every part of the country of the progress in productive efficiency. But is is useful in highlighting the wide divergences among various parts of the country in levels of income per capita.

TABLE 8

State and Regional Differences in Income Per Capita
and in Income Composition
(based on averages of ratios for 1919-21 and 1934-38)

STATE OR REGION	RATIO OF STATE PER CAPITA TO NATIONAL PER CAPITA (1)	% OF INCOME FROM NON-AGRICULTURAL INDUSTRIES (2)	% OF INCOME FROM PROPERTY (3)	% OF POPULATION REPRESENTED ON FEDERAL INCOME TAX RETURNS (4)
1 Mississippi	0.40	60.41	8.84	2.46
2 Arkansas	0.47	65.43	9.68	3.20
3 Alabama	0.47	75.16	9.09	3.44
4 South Carolina	0.50	69.38	9.26	3.31
5 Georgia	0.54	75.97	11.30	4.36
6 North Carolina	0.55	69.60	10.42	3.20
7 Tennessee	0.56	79.23	10.82	4.73
8 Kentucky	0.58	79.25	11.94	4.99
9 Louisiana	0.64	83.08	14.51	6.22
10 North Dakota	0.66	60.02	7.32	5.87
11 Virginia	0.66	82.84	12.74	6.58
12 New Mexico	0.68	72.34	8.60	6.23
13 Oklahoma	0.70	77.15	14.56	6.19
14 South Dakota	0.73	63.96	9.04	7.40
15 Florida	0.74	86.18	17.92	7.26
16 West Virginia	0.75	90.11	11.71	8.26
17 Texas	0.76	76.94	16.06	7.65
18 Iowa	0.82	73.70	13.39	9.55
19 Nebraska	0.83	74.67	13.91	10.39
20 Utah	0.83	81.68	10.32	9.79
21 Kansas	0.84	75.48	13.29	8.36
22 Idaho	0.87	65.14	8.20	8.85
23 Missouri	0.88	87.84	15.18	8.69
24 Minnesota	0.88	82.19	14.28	9.88
25 Indiana	0.88	87.04	11.38	9.32
26 Vermont	0.90	79.94	15.43	9.06
27 Maine	0.92	87.14	16.86	9.42
28 Wisconsin	0.93	79.38	11.91	10.18
29 Arizona	0.96	83.11	10.78	11.00
30 Montana	1.00	75.98	9.44	13.24
31 Colorado	1.02	83.28	15.12	11.88
32 New Hampshire	1.06	93.14	21.10	12.32
33 Oregon	1.06	81.52	11.76	12.83
34 Ohio	1.08	92.67	14.61	12.04
35 Michigan	1.09	91.56	13.29	12.37
36 Maryland	1.10	94.14	21.24	16.61
37 Pennsylvania	1.10	95.86	17.72	12.89
38 Washington	1.12	85.72	12.72	15.44
39 Illinois	1.21	93.26	17.40	14.82
40 New Jersey	1.22	97.44	19.90	16.19
41 Wyoming	1.24	72.82	10.67	17.17
42 Rhode Island	1.30	98.58	23.36	14.56
43 Delaware	1.30	92.64	30.45	14.46
44 Connecticut	1.32	96.38	23.86	17.87
45 Massachusetts	1.36	98.27	21.96	17.34
46 Nevada	1.42	83.52	13.00	21.99
47 California	1.46	88.62	19.63	18.56
48 New York	1.62	97.02	23.28	17.91
49 New England	1.27	96.25	21.84	15.74
50 North Central	1.16	93.96	14.30	13.37
51 South	0.63	78.63	13.68	5.80
52 Mountain & Plains	0.86	74.87	11.83	9.71
53 Pacific	1.34	87.38	17.66	17.20

such an association is not unexpected. It must be taken into account in interpreting differences in average income in terms of differences in living standards: some of the disparities in monetary levels are offset by disparities in living costs.

Another aspect of composition that explains state differences in income level is the distribution by type. In general, a high income per capita is associated with a relatively high proportion of income from property—interest, dividends, rent; and a low level with a relatively high proportion of income in the form of compensation for effort—wages and salaries, entrepreneurial income; the coefficient of rank correlation between columns 1 and 3 is 0.65. Naturally, there is also association between the proportion of income from nonagricultural industries and from property (col. 2 and 3); the coefficient of rank correlation is 0.83.

Finally, we can get some notion of the relative proportion of high income recipients by comparing the number of persons represented on federal income tax returns with the total population of the state. This ratio does not reflect accurately the contrast between incomes in the top brackets and those of the

Notes to Table 8

COLUMN

1 The ratio of the state or regional per capita to the national per capita for 1919-21 averaged with that for 1934-38. Per capitas for these two periods are from a manuscript by Donald Murray of the University of Pennsylvania, 'Changes in the Distribution of Income by States, 1840-1938'. The income data used by Mr. Murray are from Maurice Leven, *Income in the Various States* (National Bureau of Economic Research, 1925) and the various publications on state income payments by the Department of Commerce for recent years.

2 & 3 The percentage of income from nonagricultural industries or from property for 1919-21 averaged with that for 1934-38. Percentages for these two periods are given in or calculated from the source indicated for col. 1.

4 The number of persons represented on federal income tax returns is estimated annually for 1919-21 and for 1934-38 from the number of returns given in *Statistics of Income* and the ratio for the entire country of persons per return, as computed for *Some Aspects of the Distribution of Income by Size,* now in preparation. Averages are calculated for 1919-21 and for 1934-38 and related to the population series basic to col. 1. The percentages for the two periods are then averaged.

The state composition of regions, the same as used in Table 9, is:
New England: lines 27, 32, 26, 45, 42, and 44.
North Central: lines 48, 40, 37, 34, 25, 39, 35, 28, 24, 18, and 23.
South: lines 43, 36, 11, 16, 6, 4, 5, 15, 8, 7, 3, 1, 2, 9, 13, and 17.
Mountain & Plains: lines 10, 14, 19, 21, 30, 22, 41, 31, 12, 29, 20, and 46.
Pacific: lines 38, 33, and 47.

mass of low and middle recipients, since only numbers rather than both numbers and incomes are compared; moreover, the number of persons represented on tax returns is estimated on the basis of countrywide ratios of persons per return, rather than upon specific state ratios. Yet we may assume that filers of federal returns receive much higher incomes than the average for the state; and that the larger the income tax population the greater the inequality in the income distribution as determined by the relative proportion of recipients of income well above the average.[6]

The association between level of income per capita and inequality as measured by the percentage of the population represented on federal returns is close, the coefficient of rank correlation being 0.98. There is association also between the percentage of the population represented on federal returns and the proportion of income from nonagricultural industries or from property: the coefficients of rank correlation are 0.69 and 0.60, respectively.

Since the relative weight of agriculture is an important determinant of income per capita, we can assume that differences between rural and urban areas as well as among urban communities of different size must also be substantial. While there are no continuous data on community-size differences, the 1935-36 sample study suggests the order of magnitudes (Table 9).

In the five regions differences in income per family (either median or mean) are the same as indicated by the state data: the South and the Mountain and Plains region are characterized by distinctly lower levels than New England, the North Central, or the Pacific region, whereas differences among the latter three are relatively minor (Table 9, lines 1-5, col. 2 and 3). But when we analyze each region by community-size groups we see that the regional disparities are due almost entirely to differences in per family income in farm areas alone

[6]Table 8 is based upon data for 1919-21 and 1934-38, when exemption limits in federal income taxation were quite generous; so that filers represented groups far above the arithmetic mean income, even in states with relatively high income per capita.

TABLE 9

Characteristics of Family Income Distributions
Regions and Community-size Groups, 1935-1936

Part A   Regions and Community-size Groups Treated Separately

REGIONS AND COMMUNITY-SIZE GROUPS	NO. OF FAMILIES (mill.) (1)	MEDIAN INCOME ($) (2)	ARITHMETIC MEAN INCOME ($) (3)	RATIO OF MEAN TO MEDIAN (4)	% OF FAMILIES WITHIN 75-125% of Median (5)	50-150% of Median (6)
Regions—All Families						
1 New England	2.0	1,230	1,810	1.47	34.8	62.6
2 North Central	14.6	1,260	1,786	1.42	31.3	57.9
3 South	8.8	905	1,326	1.47	24.5	49.1
4 Mountain & Plains	1.9	1,040	1,363	1.31	27.0	52.1
5 Pacific	2.1	1,335	1,775	1.33	31.5	60.1
Community-size Groups—Nonrelief Families						
6 Metropolises	(3.3)2.8	1,730	2,704	1.56	34.5	62.3
7 Large cities	(5.6)4.7	1,560	2,177	1.40	31.8	60.1
8 Middle sized cities	(3.2)2.6	1,360	1,813	1.33	32.1	60.9
9 Small cities	(4.9)4.1	1,290	1,653	1.28	31.7	59.1
10 Rural nonfarm	(5.7)4.6	1,210	1,607	1.33	31.3	57.6
11 Farms	(6.8)6.2	965	1,259	1.30	29.1	56.2

Part B   Regions and Community-size Groups, Cross-classified (nonrelief families)

COMMUNITY-SIZE GROUPS AND ITEMS	New England (1)	North Central (2)	South (3)	Mountain & Plains (4)	Pacific (5)
Number of Families (millions)					
12 Metropolises	...	2.81	...	...	...
13 Large cities	0.48	2.07	1.15	0.18	0.78
14 Middle sized cities	0.37	1.39	0.57	0.10	0.18
15 Small cities	0.36	2.05	1.06	0.28	0.32
16 Rural nonfarm	0.25	1.88	1.74	0.41	0.31
17 Farms	0.15	2.13	3.10	0.54	0.25
Median Income (dollars)					
18 Metropolises	...	1,730	...	...	...
19 Large cities	1,361	1,646	1,484	1,607	1,544
20 Middle sized cities	1,326	1,370	1,271	1,571	1,392
21 Small cities	1,419	1,293	1,094	1,493	1,545
22 Rural nonfarm	1,457	1,163	1,159	1,341	1,433
23 Farms	1,184	1,236	780	860	1,349
% of Families within 75-125% of Median					
24 Metropolises	...	34.5	...	...	...
25 Large cities	33.6	34.6	24.8	32.2	34.3
26 Middle sized cities	36.9	34.5	20.4	39.7	36.9
27 Small cities	37.6	33.4	25.3	33.7	36.4
28 Rural nonfarm	39.2	37.0	23.8	32.9	36.8
29 Farms	36.1	35.9	31.4	26.7	28.4

LINE

1-11 Based on distributions, 1935-36, in *Consumer Incomes in the United States,*
particularly Table 10A, p. 75; Table 6, p. 22; Table 7, p. 23; Table 12B,
p. 98; and Table 9B, p. 97. Entries in parentheses in col. 1, lines 6-11, are
the numbers of families (in millions), including relief.

(Notes to Table 9 concluded on page 28)

and to the greater prevalence of these low income areas in some regions than in others (lines 18-23). Although income per family is lowest in the South for every community-size group except large cities, in the Mountain and Plains region only farm family income, and somewhat less consistently, rural nonfarm is lower. In urban communities average income per family in the Mountain and Plains region is not lower than in other regions. Again, in the South and in the Mountain and Plains region the proportion of farm families, whose incomes are usually low, is greater than in other regions: over 40 percent in the South and over 35 percent in the Mountain and Plains region, as compared with less than 10 percent in New England, somewhat over 15 percent in the North Central, and almost 15 percent in the Pacific region (see lines 12-17).

Thus, in terms of the groups in Table 9, the community-size differences in income levels appear more prominent and more consistent than the regional. Income per family declines consistently as we pass from the very large urban communities to the smaller cities, to rural nonfarm areas, and finally to farms (lines 6-11, col. 2 and 3). There is similar consistency in the Mountain and Plains region and, in less degree, in the North Central and the South (lines 18-23, col. 2 and 3); and even in the other regions income per farm family is lower than income per family in all other community-size groups.

Both regions and community-size groups show the expected marked skewness to the right in the distribution of family income. It is more appreciable in New England, the North Central region, and the South than in the Mountain and Plains, and the Pacific region (lines 1-5, col. 4). More significant perhaps is the fact that it diminishes as we pass from the big cities to the smaller, then rises as we pass to the rural communi-

Notes to Table 9 concluded
The population ranges for the nonfarm communities (lines 6-10) are:

Metropolises	1,500,000 and over
Large cities	100,000 to 1,500,000
Middle sized cities	25,000 to 100,000
Small cities	2,500 to 25,000
Rural nonfarm communities	Under 2,500

12-18 From *ibid.*, Table 24B, p. 101, and Table 7, p. 23.
19-29 Calculated from distributions in *ibid.*, Tables 14B-18B, pp. 98-9.

ties and farms (lines 6-11, col. 4). The bigger the city the more opportunity obviously for families with incomes large enough to extend the right tail of the distribution—an expected corollary of the greater importance in these larger cities of pursuits that afford a likelihood for such very high incomes (independent professional practice and business). In the nonurban areas the absence of a large employee class may contribute to greater skewness.

Inequality in distribution by size as measured by the proportion of families whose incomes are 25 or 50 percent above or below the median income, is greatest in the regions with the largest proportion of farm or rural families—the South and the Mountain and Plains region (lines 1-5, col. 5 and 6); these are also the regions where the difference betw :en farm and nonfarm family incomes is greatest (lines 18-23). Measured similarly for community-size groups, inequality is greatest among farm families and least in metropolitan communities (lines 6-11, col. 5 and 6).

When we cross-classify regions and community-size groups, the greater range of differences among family incomes in the South is true of most community-size groups (lines 24-29), but no other interregional difference in family income inequality appears consistently. Curiously enough, there is also little consistency in intercommunity-size group differences in the inequality of family income. Perhaps the data and the measures are not sensitive enough to reveal them.

The general impression of this analysis of income by states, regions, and community-size groups is the dominance of the rural-urban differential in levels of per capita or per family income, and the additional association between these levels and the proportion of income from property. As far as dispersion or inequality is concerned, a wide variety of factors seems active, no one of which is outstanding, at least in the data and measures available. In some regions inequality is greater in rural areas than in urban; in others it is less. In some regions, notably the South where the disparity in income between white and negro families is wide, inequality is consistently greater than in other regions, for most community-size groups. The size distribution of income is like an enormous mosaic made up of regional, community-size, occupational, industrial, and noneconomic (race, nativity, etc.) group differences. All affect the income level and the characteristics of its distribution within any considerable population group. Indeed, in the distribution of income among individuals and families, we are at a point where the functioning of the economy impinges directly upon the activities and lives of the millions and where the variety of factors that determine their manifold grouping begins to be reflected in numerous differentials in income levels and dispersions. At this point analysis cannot be pushed much further without the assistance of what, for want of a better term, might be designated economic sociology, concerned with the anatomy and physiology of social groupings, whose characteristics affect the income receipts and disbursements of their members.

PART II

Long Term Changes, 1869—1938

National income is the earnings of current effort applied to accumulated assets, tangible and intangible. The skills and facilities employed in producing it are a heritage from the past, improved in the present, and passed on to the future. Long term changes in it indicate how this country reached the levels enjoyed in the immediate past and afford a basis for judging the prospects of a continuation of its growth.

Information needed to trace long term changes in national income and its composition is more scanty than that for recent years; and the estimates for a more distant past are subject to a wider margin of error than those for years beginning with 1919. Nevertheless, estimates of national income by final use categories can be constructed to form a continuous series of decade averages, overlapping by five-year periods, from 1869-78 through 1929-38. From other estimates we can get some notion of long term changes in the distribution by industrial origin and by type of payment. While these series could be continued through 1944, it seemed better to stop with 1938, for the interpretation of war production, the chief influence since 1940, in terms of the secular growth of the economy is difficult. In a few years a better view of the extent to which the prewar trends have continued or were modified can be attained.[7]

1 *Total and Per Capita*

The decade estimates of national income, total and per capita, in Table 10, present a long record of growth in the country's

[7]For a discussion of the problems of measuring national income in wartime and an analysis of the estimates for World Wars I and II see *National Product in Wartime* (National Bureau of Economic Research, 1945).

31

TABLE 10

National Income, 1929 Prices, Total and Per Capita
Decade Estimates, 1869-1938

	AVERAGE PER YEAR			% CHANGE FROM DECADE		
	National Income ($ bill.)	Population (mill.)	Per Capita ($)	TO OVERLAPPING DECADE		
DECADE				National Income	Population	Per Capita
	(1)	(2)	(1)÷(2) (3)	(4)	(5)	(6)
1 1869-78	9.3	43.5	215			
2 1874-83	13.6	48.8	278	+45.6	+12.2	+29.3
3 1879-88	17.9	54.8	326	+31.4	+12.1	+17.3
4 1884-93	21.0	61.2	344	+17.7	+11.7	+5.5
5 1889-98	24.2	67.6	357	+14.9	+10.6	+3.8
6 1894-03	29.8	74.3	401	+23.1	+9.8	+12.3
7 1899-08	37.3	81.5	458	+25.5	+9.8	+14.2
8 1904-13	45.0	89.6	502	+20.5	+9.9	+9.6
9 1909-18	50.6	97.7	517	+12.4	+9.0	+3.0
10 1914-23	57.3	105.0	546	+13.3	+7.4	+5.6
11 1919-28	69.0	112.8	612	+20.6	+7.5	+12.1
12 1924-33	73.3	120.6	607	+6.1	+6.9	—0.8
13 1929-38	72.0	126.0	572	—1.7	+4.4	—5.8
Averages (geometric means)						
14 Lines 2-13				+18.6	+9.3	+8.5
15 2- 5				+26.8	+11.6	+13.5
16 6- 9				+20.3	+9.6	+9.7
17 10-13				+9.3	+6.5	+2.6
18 2- 5				+26.8	+11.6	+13.5
19 5- 8				+20.9	+10.0	+9.9
20 8-11				+16.6	+8.5	+7.5

COLUMN
ŧ *National Product since 1869,* Table II 16, col. 10.
2 Averages of annual estimates in *Statistical Abstract, 1942,* p. 11.

product. The percentage rates of change from one decade to the next in columns 4-6 reveal clearly the three aspects of long term growth that quantitative records usually exhibit: the average rate of increase; its retardation; and the long swings, variously designated as secondary secular movements, trend-cycles, or long cycles. We discuss below the average rate of growth and the retardation in it, leaving the subject of trend-cycles to the last Section of this Part.

Since 1869, national income has grown at the rate of almost 19 percent per quinquennium; population at over 8 percent; income per capita at 8.5 percent (line 14). The cumulative effect of these rates is evident in the change from the midpoint of the first decade, 1869-78, to that of the last, 1929-

38: national income multiplying almost eightfold; population and income per capita almost tripling. Even if our estimates understate the true level of national income by as much as 10 percent in 1869-78 and 5 percent in 1874-83,[8] national income would still show a rise to seven times its level in the first decade of the period; and income per capita to a level about two and a half times that for 1869-78.

Whether such a rise in six decades is unusual can be judged partly from a comparison with the long term experience of other countries, partly from the experience of this country at other times. By either standard it was among the highest. Of the four countries for which we have rough estimates for an equally long recent period—Great Britain, Sweden, Germany, France—Sweden alone shows approximately the same rate. However, countries that began to industrialize later, notably Japan and the USSR, have higher rates, if over somewhat shorter periods.[9] Nevertheless, a record such as is shown in Table 10 is matched only by the kind of secular growth characteristic of a period of rapid industrialization.

Comparisons with growth in this country's past afford other confirmatory evidence. Estimates for the years preceding the Civil War (back to 1800) can be only of the crudest. But they indicate that with respect to the growth of national income and of income per capita (but not of population), the rates for the recent six decades are distinctly higher than those between 1800 and 1860.[10]

Though the rates of growth of national income, total and per capita, are high, one must not overstress their significance as measures of increase in capacity to produce or in economic welfare. That income per capita rose from less than $250 in 1869-78 to about $600 in 1919-38 (col. 3) does not mean that the average capacity to produce rose by the same ratio; or that on the average the people of this country were over

[8] For a more detailed discussion of this possible understatement see *National Product since 1869* (National Bureau of Economic Research, 1946), Part II, Sec. 1-4.

[9] Colin Clark gives estimates for various countries in *Conditions of Economic Progress,* particularly Ch. IV.

[10] See Robert F. Martin, *National Income in the United States, 1799-1938* (National Industrial Conference Board, 1939), Table 1, pp. 6-7.

twice as well-off in the 1920's as in the 1870's. Between the beginning and end of the period covered in Table 10 basic conditions of work and life changed too greatly for the quantitative differences in dollar value estimates, even at constant prices, to have exact meaning in terms of productive performance or economic welfare. Technological changes in conditions of work have meant not so much increased capacity to produce the same things with less effort as capacity to produce things that could not be made earlier—products that either satisfy already established wants more satisfactorily or cater to new tastes and desires. It is, therefore, difficult to make exact comparisons of productive performance, even between a mule and a tractor—let alone between a horse and an airplane. And it is equally difficult to compare the welfare significance of various goods to an urban dweller in the twentieth century and to a village dweller of the 1870's. Such comparisons are possible only by applying criteria of technical performance or human well-being that are outside the changing short term viewpoints of the market place whence economists derive their yardsticks. One can say only that the record in Table 10 indicates large growth in product per capita, in the country's capacity to produce, even when measured per member of its vastly greater population. Presumably this means a substantial increase in economic welfare or power per capita—but exactly how much cannot be said.

That the rate of growth declined is clearly suggested by the entries in columns 4-6. Fluctuations, to be discussed below, obscure the general downward trend; but the latter is revealed when figures are averaged. The averages in lines 15-17, grouping the decades that are comprised in the distinguishable long swings, reveal the decline in the rate of growth clearly; in total national income from about 27 percent per quinquennium in the first part of the period to about 9 percent in the last part; in population from about 12 to 6.5 percent; in income per capita from 13.5 to less than 3 percent. An adjustment for maximum possible understatement in the first two decades does not change the picture materially: it reduces the geometric mean for total national income in line 15 to 23.5 percent and for income per capita to 10.7 percent. Likewise, if we fit a straight line (by the method of least squares) to the percentage rates of increase in columns 4-6 (converted to logarithms), we find that for the period as a whole the lines slope downward, indicating retardation.[11]

Even if we exclude the last two decades as severely affected by the depression of 1929-32, and regroup the remaining entries in sets of four with one overlapping, the average percentage increase in national income drops to 17 percent per quinquennium in the last period from either 27 or 23.5 in the first, as we discard or accept the maximum adjustment for understatement: in population to 8.5 percent from 11.6; and in income per capita to 7.5 percent from either 13.5 or 10.7.

The significance for the future of this retardation in the rate of growth is more easily assessed for total national income and population than for income per capita. It does not seem likely that growth in the former two during the next six decades will be of the same relative magnitude as that from 1869-78 to 1929-38. Statements concerning a country's economic future are always hazardous. But there are no signs that the population of this country will triple during the next sixty years as it did between the early 1870's and early 1930's. Indeed, recent estimates put the total in the 1990's at about 167 million—a rise of only 33 percent from the 1929-38 decade; and assume a rate of growth per quinquennium that will be materially lower in the immediate future (2.5 percent) than it was during 1914-38 (6.5), and will drop gradually to almost zero by 1995.[12] Under such conditions of population growth, even a constant rate of increase in income per capita would mean a declining rate of growth in total national income. Unless income per capita showed a tendency toward

---

[11] These lines were fitted to the series in Table 10 and to the estimates for components in order to bring out more clearly the timing and amplitude of fluctuations in the rates of growth. For the constants see Tables 19-21.

[12] See *Estimates of Future Population of the United States, 1940-2000* (National Resources Planning Board, Washington, D. C., 1943), Table 8, p. 74. We chose the figures based on the assumption of medium fertility, medium mortality, with no immigration, no war losses.

an accelerated rate of increase sufficient to compensate for the
decline in the rate of population growth, total national income would continue to increase at a declining rate. If continued long enough, this would mean reaching a limit beyond
which only insignificant growth could take place. In any event,
it is unlikely that national income, during the coming sixty
years, will multiply eightfold, as it did between the early
1870's and early 1930's: for that would entail a rise in per
capita income exceeding that in this country, or probably else-
where, during an equally long period.

The prospect that neither population nor national income
will grow in the future at the high rate of the sixty years
preceding World War II; or even that their growth is likely
to be at increasingly slower rates as compared with the last
part of the sixty years covered in Table 10 is disturbing only
if one considers a population and total product much larger
than the present an assurance of the country's survival in a
hostile world. Disregarding such considerations, whose validity
can scarcely be judged here, one may doubt that a high rate
of population growth in the future is compatible with the maintenance or desirable increase of income per capita. A population
of over 350 million (i.e., three times that of 1929-38) by
the early 1990's could be sustained at the present income and
hence standard of living per capita only if a technological
revolution of a scope wider even than that suggested by such
recent events as the atomic bomb occurred. And the maintenance of the rate of increase of even the depressed 1930's
(4.4 percent per quinquennium, Table 10, line 13, col. 5)
would bring the population to over 210 million by the early
1990's.

If we disregard questions of desirability but grant the
prospects of a slower growth of population and possibly of
total national income, what is the implication of the record
of income per capita? If the population grows more slowly,
will income per capita also? Or will the slower growth of
population permit a more rapid increase in income per capita
than in the past?

The record does not indicate as great a decline in the first part of the period in the rate of growth of income per capita as in that of population and of total income. An adjustment for maximum understatement in 1869-78 and 1874-83 lowers the average rate of growth in lines 15 and 18 (col. 6) to 10.7 percent, reducing the drop to the average for the middle part of the sixty year span (lines 16 and 19). The rate of increase drops materially in the last part of the period (to 2.6 percent) when we include the decade of the depressed 1930's; not so much (to 7.5 percent) when we exclude that decade. All in all, however, the record suggests a retardation in the rate of growth of income per capita, but at a more moderate pace than in total national income.

Continuation of past trends would thus mean a decline in the rate of growth in national income per capita, moderate, or sizable depending upon our judgment of the secular significance of the 1929-32 depression and of the incomplete recovery from it. But whether we can assume a continuance of the trends shown in Table 10 depends partly upon the validity of taking 1869-1938 as the base, partly upon the continuance of the type of social organization and the drives that have characterized this country. One could argue that the period chosen tends to exaggerate retardation in long term growth because it begins with the intensive reconstruction shortly after the Civil War and ends with the severe depression of the 1930's. Also, changes that would provide new incentives and new possibilities for either accelerated growth or at least for growth at rates not below those of the recent past are not out of the question. The very retardation of the rate of increase in population is, in a country with necessarily limited resources, a factor favorable to higher levels of per capita product; and a combination of a very moderate rate of growth in population with a high rate of growth in income per capita has been observed in the past (e.g., in Sweden). On the other hand, it not difficult to find factors that would brake the rate of growth in income per capita even more than is suggested by Table 10. No conclusive answer can be given here. While summarizing some aspects of our economic experience for a long period and reflecting the continuous operation of institutions that are likely to survive and to exhibit the changing pattern they have during the long term past, the estimates contribute only one datum of importance in evaluating the probable lines of growth of the economy. Before they can yield a reasonable prognosis of the future, they must be supplemented by direct consideration and evaluation of the factors that made for growth and retardation in the past.

One must be particularly wary of interpreting retardation in secular growth observed in the past, or even its extrapolation to the future, as verifying theories of economic maturity or secular stagnation that have become current recently. One may and should grant that data for the past, such as the estimates presented above, indicate a distinct retardation in the rate of growth in population, national income, and income per capita. Given the forecasts of future population characterized by a marked damping of growth, and the failure of experience to show long term acceleration in the rate of growth in income per capita, one may reasonably infer that a retarded rate of growth is likely also in total national income, if not unavoidably in income per capita. But these inferences are not uniquely related to such theses of the theory of secular stagnation as the prospective shortage of private investment opportunities relative to the amount of monetary savings to be generated; the prospect of chronic secular unemployment; or the policy conclusions as to the need for public investment drawn from the theses just stated. One could easily visualize a social framework within which population, income, and even income per capita would grow at decreasing rates, yet there would be no signs of a shortage of private investment opportunities, chronic unemployment, etc. On the contrary, one could just as easily visualize a situation in which these latter phenomena would occur while the rate of increase in population, national income, and income per capita was accelerating. In other words, proof of these particular theses in the theory of secular stagnation requires data quite different from those yielded by estimates of national income; and the association between retardation in the long term growth of national income and the theses concerning

shortages of private investment opportunities and the likelihood of rising levels of secular unemployment can be demonstrated only by an analysis of the factors that brought about
growth and retardation in the past and are likely to continue. In this sense, the mere observation of retardation in
the rate of growth in the past and its simple extrapolation into the future no more constitutes a proof of the theory of
secular stagnation than the observation and extrapolation of
constant or accelerating rates of growth would constitute a
disproof.

2 *Distribution by Industrial Origin*

The rapid growth in national income and population during
the sixty years before World War II was partly a concomitant,
partly a result of the process of industrialization. In the early
phases of industrialization the relative distribution of resources and product shifted to the secondary industries, such
as mining and manufacturing, and to transportation and other
utilities. In the later phases, at least in this country, it shifted
toward the service industries.

While the estimates of the distribution of national income
(or of a closely related total, aggregate payments) by industrial origin back to 1869 in Table 11 suffer from lack of
comparability, certain long term trends in the industrial structure of national income stand out. Though the share of
agriculture in 1869 and 1879 was moderate, 20.5 percent, it
had declined to less than half by 1929-38. The shares of
mining and manufacturing rose at first; but in the last two
or three decades of the period apparently did not rise further.
The share of construction declined during the period as a
whole. Transportation and other public utilities, surprisingly
enough, account for a slightly declining, rather than a rising,
share—owing, perhaps, to a secular decline in prices of transportation and of other utility services greater than that
in prices of goods produced by other industries. In view of
the crudity of the estimates, the rather small decline in the
share of trade cannot be accorded too much significance. The
share of service declined somewhat from high levels in the

TABLE 11

National Income and Aggregate Payments
Percentage Distribution by Industry, 1869-1938
(based on values in current prices)

	AGR. (1)	MINING (2)	MFG. (3)	CON-STRUC-TION (4)	TRANSP. & OTHER PUBLIC UTILITIES (5)	TRADE (6)	SERVICE (7)	GOV. (8)	FINANCE & MISC. (9)
	Based on Martin's Estimates of Aggregate Payments								
AVERAGE OF									
1 1869 & 1879	20.5	1.8	13.9	5.3	11.9	15.7	14.7	4.4	11.7
2 1879 & 1889	16.1	2.1	16.6	5.5	11.9	16.6	13.6	4.9	12.6
3 1889 & 1899	17.1	2.5	18.2	4.9	10.7	16.8	11.8	6.0	12.0
DECADE									
4 1899-08	16.7	3.1	18.4	4.5	10.7	15.3	9.6	5.6	16.0
5 1904-13	17.0	3.3	18.9	4.3	11.0	15.0	8.9	5.4	16.2
6 1909-18	17.7	3.3	20.8	3.2	10.7	14.5	8.2	6.3	15.4
7 1914-23	15.2	3.3	22.2	3.0	11.0	14.0	8.3	7.9	15.0
8 1919-28	12.2	3.1	22.2	3.9	11.3	13.7	9.4	8.6	15.7
DECADE	*Based on NBER Estimates of National Income*								
9 1919-28	10.5	2.5	21.9	4.4	9.8	13.6	11.6	9.6	16.1
10 1924-33	8.7	1.9	19.6	4.2	10.4	13.3	13.4	11.8	16.7
11 1929-38	8.5	1.7	19.4	2.9	10.0	13.6	13.9	14.4	15.6

LINE

1-8 Based on estimates in R. F. Martin, *National Income in the United States, 1799-1938* (National Industrial Conference Board, 1939), particularly Tables 1, 16, 40, 43, and 46. Mr. Martin's 'total realized income' is most comparable with our total of aggregate payments (excl. entrepreneurial savings). 'Miscellaneous income of private origin' (see Table 43), largely rent, and 'net international transfers of dividends and interest' (Table 46) were included in the 'finance and miscellaneous' category. In lines 1-3 rents are distributed among the various industries; in lines 4-8 they are included under 'finance and miscellaneous'.

9-11 Averages of annual estimates in *National Income and Its Composition*, Vol. One, Table 59.

1870's and 1880's, then remained fairly stable, and rose appreciably in the 1920's and 1930's. The share of government rose consistently throughout the period, but that of finance (including miscellaneous) changed little—the rise in line 4 over line 3 being due, in all probability, to the change in the treatment of rent. The outstanding basic shifts are the decline in the share of agriculture, the rise, then stability of the shares of mining and manufacturing, and the rise of the combined category of the service industries (a total of service, government, and finance).

The distributions in Table 11 are for national income and

aggregate payments in current prices; and differences among the secular movements of prices of the goods produced by the several industries may affect trends in the apportionment by industrial origin. No differential price adjustment that would yield long term changes in the industrial composition of national income in constant prices is possible. But a continuous series of the industrial distribution of the gainfully occupied indicates the shifting importance of various industries, judged not by their contributions to real national product but by their relative shares in the most important productive resource—manpower. Table 12 shows most of the basic

TABLE 12
Gainfully Occupied and Employed
Percentage Distribution by Industry, 1870-1940

	AGR. (1)	MINING (2)	MFG. (3)	CONSTRUCTION (4)	TRANSP. & OTHER PUBLIC UTILITIES (5)	TRADE (6)	FINANCE (7)	GOV. (8)	SERVICE & MISC. (9)
YEAR			G A I N	F U L L Y	O C C U	P I E D			
1 1870	51.6	1.5	16.4	5.4	4.3	6.3	0.4	1.9	12.4
2 1880	48.8	1.8	18.3	4.9	4.6	7.1	0.4	2.2	11.9
3 1890	42.5	2.0	19.3	5.9	5.9	8.1	0.7	2.5	13.2
4 1900	37.7	2.6	21.3	5.6	6.6	9.0	1.1	2.7	13.3
5 1910	30.7	2.9	21.9	6.2	8.0	9.7	1.5	3.4	15.7
6 1920	26.7	2.9	25.5	5.2	9.2	10.0	1.9	4.3	14.1
7 1930	21.3	2.4	22.3	6.2	9.1	12.7	3.0	4.9	18.1
8 1940	16.9	2.1	22.4	6.6	7.2	13.3	2.9	5.5	23.1
DECADE			E M	P L O Y	E D				
9 1919-28	20.6	2.6	22.8	4.0	8.0	14.0	2.7	7.2	18.1
10 1924-33	20.2	2.3	20.9	3.9	7.2	14.6	3.1	7.6	20.1
11 1929-38	20.6	2.2	20.6	2.9	6.1	14.4	3.2	8.5	21.5

LINE

1-8 Based on estimates made by Daniel Carson for 'Labor Supply and Employment' (WPA, National Research Project, Nov. 1939, mimeo.) and revised in 'Industrial Composition of Manpower in the United States, 1870-1940', a paper prepared for the Conference on Research in Income and Wealth, 1945.

9-11 Averages of annual estimates in *National Income and Its Composition*, Vol. One, Table 69. For definition of 'employed' see note to Table 2.

trends already suggested in Table 11, but much more conspicuously. The share of agriculture in the gainfully occupied drops from over one-half in 1870 to about one-sixth in 1940. The shares of mining and manufacturing rise until about 1920, then become stable or decline slightly—a trend observable also in the share of construction, if we disregard the depression decade 1929-38. The proportion of transportation and other public utilities rises, sharply and consistently, until the last decade, confirming the suggestion advanced above that the decline in the share of this category in aggregate payments in current prices (in Table 11) may be due largely to the greater secular decline in prices of transportation and of other public utility services. The proportions of trade, finance, government, and the service and miscellaneous industries all show an unmistakable secular rise, the rise in the shares of the industries concerned with rendering services rather than producing or transporting commodities being more pronounced in the second half of the long period than in the first.

By combining the data on the growth of national income in Table 10, the number of the gainfully occupied underlying Table 12, its industrial distribution, and assuming inter-industry differences in income per gainfully occupied, we can spot some factors contributing to the growth of national income in constant prices. We exclude from this analysis the decades after 1919-28: our long series in Table 12 being for the gainfully occupied rather than the employed, the inclusion of the last two decades with their unusually heavy unemployment would distort the result. And we assume that throughout the period inter-industry differences in income per gainfully occupied are of the same relative magnitude as those in income per employed 1919-38 (Table 2, col. 5). This assumption involves possible errors due to: (1) substituting ratios per employed for ratios per gainfully occupied; and (2) assuming constancy over time in inter-industry differences in income per gainfully occupied. The first error is minor, as can be seen by comparing the percentage shares in Table 12, lines 9-11, with those in lines 7-8: the disparities are not of a kind that would materially affect differences in the ratios established in Table 2, column 5. The second error may be more appreciable. Partly as a check upon the underlying assumption, partly for the interest the results might have in and of themselves, we tried to approximate the long term changes in the shares of a few industries in national income, *in constant prices* (Table 13).

TABLE 13
Percentage Shares of Selected Industries in National Income (Constant Prices) and in Gainfully Occupied, 1869-1930

		AGRICULTURE (1)	MINING (2)	MANUFACTURING (3)	CON-STRUCTION (4)	TOTAL COMMODITY PRODUCTION (5)
	DECADE	*% Shares in National Income in Constant Prices*				
1	1869-78	27.5	1.0	17.1	6.0	51.6
2	1879-88	20.5	1.2	16.3	5.7	43.7
3	1889-98	18.4	1.7	18.8	7.2	46.1
4	1899-08	15.4	2.1	19.4	5.9	42.8
5	1909-18	13.0	2.5	22.5	4.8	42.8
6	1919-28	10.5	2.5	21.9	4.4	39.3
	AVERAGE OF	*% Shares in Gainfully Occupied*				
7	1870 & 1880	50.2	1.6	17.3	5.1	74.3
8	1880 & 1890	45.6	1.9	18.8	5.4	71.7
9	1890 & 1900	40.1	2.3	20.3	5.8	68.5
10	1900 & 1910	34.2	2.7	21.6	5.9	64.4
11	1910 & 1920	28.7	2.9	23.7	5.7	61.0
12	1920 & 1930	24.0	2.7	23.9	5.7	56.3
	Ratio of Share in National Income to That in Gainfully Occupied					
13	Line 1 ÷ line 7	0.55	0.62	0.99	1.18	0.69
14	Line 2 ÷ line 8	0.45	0.63	0.87	1.06	0.61
15	Line 3 ÷ line 9	0.46	0.74	0.93	1.24	0.67
16	Line 4 ÷ line 10	0.45	0.78	0.90	1.00	0.66
17	Line 5 ÷ line 11	0.45	0.86	0.95	0.84	0.70
18	Line 6 ÷ line 12	0.44	0.93	0.92	0.77	0.70

COLUMN LINES 1-5

1-3 Line 6 extrapolated by an index of the ratio of the physical output index for the given industry to national income in 1929 prices. The latter is from *National Product since 1869*, Table II 16, col. 10. Decade averages of indexes of output are derived from the annual series indicated below.

Agriculture: For 1897-1928, from *American Agriculture, 1899-1939* by Harold Barger and Hans H. Landsberg (National Bureau of Economic Research, 1942), p. 404, extrapolated back to 1869 by the index in *Gross Farm Income and Indices of Farm Production and Prices in the United States, 1869-1937* by Frederick Strauss and Louis H. Bean (Department of Agriculture, Washington, D. C., 1940), Table 61, p. 126; the two series were spliced by the average ratio for 1897-1901.

Mining: For 1899-1928, from *The Mining Industries, 1899-1939*, by Harold Barger and Sam H. Schurr (National Bureau of Economic Research, 1944), Table A-5, p. 343, extrapolated back to 1869 by the index in *Forecasting Business Cycles* by Warren M. Persons (Wiley, 1931), Table 12, pp. 170-1; the two series were spliced by the average ratio for 1899-1904.

Manufacturing: For 1899-1928, from *The Output of Manufacturing Industries, 1899-1937* and *Employment in Manufacturing, 1899-1939* by Solomon Fabricant (National Bureau of Economic Research, 1940 and 1942), pp. 602 and 331, respectively. Extrapolation back to 1869 is by the index in *Forecasting Business Cycles*, Table 12, pp. 170-1; the two series were spliced by the average ratio for 1899-1904.

4 Line 6 extrapolated by the ratio of gross construction, 1929 prices (*National*

(Notes to Table 13 concluded on page 44)

This approximation is based upon a comparison of the index of physical output for each industry with national income, in 1929 prices. The former measures the gross output of an industry, rather than net income originating in it (i.e., the difference between gross output and payments for goods and services to other industries). The comparison, therefore, yields a good approximation to the share of a given industry in national income in constant prices only if there is no pronounced trend in the proportion of net income originating to gross output (both in constant prices). There is no way of checking upon this assumption, but comparisons of net income originating and gross value of output, in current prices, for the last three decades (1919-28, 1924-33, 1929-38) do not show marked shifts in the ratio, except for mining. Accepting the assumption,[18] we can extrapolate the percentage share of a given industry in national income in 1919-28 by an index based on the ratio of the index of physical output to national income in 1929 prices (Table 13, lines 1-6).

These calculations, which can be made only for the four commodity producing industries, show long term trends in their shares similar to those indicated by the estimates in current prices in Table 11: declines in the shares of agriculture

[18]The estimate for construction, based upon an index of total new construction rather than contract construction alone, involves an additional assumption—the constancy of the relative proportion of force account construction. This particular assumption is probably invalid, since the proportion of force account construction has increased. Yet the broad trends in the share of construction in national income should not be completely obscured by the resulting bias.

Notes to Table 13 concluded

COLUMN

    Product since 1869, Table II 5, col. 7), to gross national product, 1929 prices (*ibid.*, Table II 16, col. 9).

  5 Sum of col. 1-4.

LINE 6

1-4 Average of annual estimates of the percentage share of the given industry in national income in current prices (*National Income and Its Composition, 1919-1938,* Vol. One, Table 59).

  5 Sum of col. 1-4.

LINES 7-12

1-4 Averages of annual data in Table 12.

  5 Sum of col. 1-4.

and construction, and rises followed by stabilization in the shares of mining and manufacturing. Even the magnitudes of the trends are not too different. Yet for agriculture the decline in the share in Table 13 is appreciably larger than in Table 11; and for manufacturing the rise of the share in Table 13 is smaller than in Table 11. The comparison does not warrant identifying the trends in the apportionment of national income in current prices with those in the distribution of the total in constant prices.

The important question at the moment is whether a comparison of the shares of industries in national income (in constant prices) with their shares in the gainfully occupied reveals any decided trends in inter-industry differences in income per gainfully occupied. The answer (Table 13, lines 13-18) is that for two large industries—agriculture and manufacturing—the ratio of income per gainfully occupied to the countrywide average is fairly constant (except the drop in agriculture during the first decade). There is a distinct upward trend in this ratio for mining, and a downward trend in the ratio for construction. But these industries are small; much more significant is the near stability of the ratio of income per gainfully occupied to the countrywide average for the large group of commodity producing industries as a whole.

In the light of these findings it is not unreasonable to assume that relative inter-industry differences in income per gainfully occupied have remained fairly stable—at least for industries that loom large in the national total and thus determine its growth. We can then combine the inter-industry differences in income per employed established in Table 2, column 5, with shifts in the industrial distribution of the gainfully occupied measured in Table 12, and with data on the absolute growth of both income and gainfully occupied, distinguish several elements in the long term rise of national income.

How much of the total increase, $59 billion, in national income, 1875-1925, can be associated with the increase in the number of gainfully occupied, if we disregard any rise in income per gainfully occupied? Assigning to the increase in the

number of gainfully occupied, 30.5 million, the 1875 income
per gainfully occupied ($701, in 1929 prices), we obtain $21
billion as the income ascribable to this addition to the gainfully occupied. This leaves $38 billion, or well over 60 per-
cent of the total increase in national income, to be associated
with the increase in income per gainfully occupied (Table 14).

This secular rise in income per gainfully occupied can be
further analyzed into the rise due to the increase in income

TABLE 14

Analysis of Rise in National Income, 1875-1925
(based on values in 1929 prices)

	ABSOLUTE VALUES			CHANGE OVER PERIOD		
	1875	1900	1925	1875-1925	1875-1900	1900-25
	(1)	(2)	(3)	(4)	(5)	(6)
1 National income ($ billions)	10.6	32.0	69.5	+58.9	+21.4	+37.5
2 Gainfully occupied (millions)	15.16	29.07	45.63	+30.47	+13.91	+16.56
3 Income per gainfully occupied ($)	701	1,102	1,523	+822	+401	+421

*Increase in National Income due to Increase in Gainfully Occupied and
That due to Increase in Income per Gainfully Occupied*

4 Increase in total due to increase in gainfully occupied ($ billions)	+21.4	+9.8	+18.2
5 Line 4 as % of line 1	36.3	45.8	48.5
6 Increase in total due to increase in income per gainfully occupied ($ billions) (line 1 — line 4)	+37.5	+11.6	+19.3

Increase in National Income due to Increase in Income per Gainfully Occupied

7 Total increase in income per gainfully occupied ($) (line 3)	+822	+401	+421
8 Intra-industry increase ($)	+486	+283	+228
9 Line 8 as % of line 7	59	71	54
10 Inter-industry increase (incl. shift in inter-industry relative differentials from those in 1919-38) ($) (line 7 — line 8)	+336	+118	+193
11 Line 10 as % of line 7	41	29	46

COLUMN   LINE 1
 1-3 By straight line interpolation from Table 10.

   LINE 2
 1-3 By straight line interpolation of data underlying Table 12.

   LINE 3
 1-3 Line 1 ÷ line 2.

   LINE 4
 4 Line 2, col. 4, × line 3, col. 1.
 5 Line 2, col. 5, × line 3, col. 1.
 6 Line 2, col. 6, × line 3, col. 2.

   LINE 8
 4 Computed as follows:

COLUMN

1925

1 National income per gainfully occupied[a]   1,523

AGRICULTURE
2 % share in total gainfully occupied[b]   24.0
3 Preliminary estimate of income per gainfully
   occupied (0.5[c] × line 1)   762
4 Line 2 × line 3   18,288.0

MINING
5 % share in total gainfully occupied[b]   2.7
6 Preliminary estimate of income per gainfully
   occupied (0.9[c] × line 1)   1,371
7 Line 5 × line 6   3,701.7

8-28 MFG., CONSTRUCTION, ETC. (7 major industrial divisions)
29 Total gainfully occupied, 9 major industrial
   divisions (line 2 + line 5, etc.), %   100.0
30 Total product, 9 major industrial divisions
   (line 4 + line 7, etc.)   149,393.3
31 Weighted av., income per gainfully occupied, 9 major
   industrial divisions (line 30 ÷ line 29)   1,492
32 Adjustment factor (line 1 ÷ line 31)   1.0208

*Final Estimate of Income per Gainfully Occupied for Each
of the 9 Major Industrial Divisions*
33 Agriculture (line 3 × line 32)   778
34 Mining (line 6 × line 32)   1,400
35-41 Mfg., Construction, etc. (7 major industrial divisions)

*Calculation of 1925 on 1875 Base and Estimated Intra-industry
Increase from 1875 to 1925*

	% SHARE OF GAINFULLY OCCUPIED, 1875[b] (1)	ESTIMATED INCOME PER GAINFULLY OCCUPIED, 1925[d] (2)	(1) × (2) (3)
42 Agriculture	50.2	778	39,055.6
43 Mining	1.6	1,400	2,240.0
44-50 Mfg., Construction, etc. (7 major industrial divisions)			
51 Total, 9 major industrial divisions, (lines 42-50)	100.0		118,696.9

52 Weighted av., income per gainfully occupied,
   9 major industrial divisions (line 51, col. 3 ÷ col. 1)   1,187
53 National income per gainfully occupied, 1875[e]   701
54 Intra-industry increase (line 52 — line 53)   486

[a]Line 3, col. 3 of Table 14.
[b]By straight line interpolation from Table 12.
[c]Table 2, col. 5.
[d]Lines 33-41.
[e]Line 3, col. 1 of Table 14.
5 & 6 Computed by a procedure paralleling that for col. 4.

per gainfully occupied within each of the nine major industrial
categories in Table 12 (intra-industry rise); and the rise due
to the shift in the distribution of the gainfully occupied from
industries in which income per gainfully occupied is below the
countrywide average (e.g., in agriculture) to those in which
it is above (e.g., transportation and other public utilities). Of
the total rise in income per gainfully occupied, $822 (in 1929
prices), $486, or 59 percent, was due to the intra-industry rise
in income per gainfully occupied, and $336, or 41 percent, to
the shifts from industries with lower to industries with higher
income per gainfully occupied.[14]

In columns 5 and 6 a similar analysis is carried through
separately for each half of the fifty years. In general, the
increase in national income, in the gainfully occupied, and in
income per gainfully occupied is, in absolute terms, larger
from 1900 to 1925. But in percentage terms, it is distinctly
smaller: in national income it is 117 percent of the 1900 base
as compared with 202 percent of the 1875 base; in the gainfully occupied, 57 percent as compared with 92 percent; in
income per gainfully occupied, 38 percent as compared with
57 percent. Thus crudely halving the full period brings out the
retardation in the percentage secular rise in national income,
population, and per capita income, shown in somewhat greater
detail in Table 10.

For each of the two quarter centuries, somewhat less than
half of the total rise in national income may be associated
with the growth in the gainfully occupied and the remaining
portion with the increase in the income per gainfully occupied.
Of the latter, 71 percent during the first twenty-five years and
54 percent during the second is due to the intra-industry rise;
and 29 and 46 percent respectively to the shifts from industries with lower levels of income per gainfully occupied to
industries with higher levels (inter-industry shift). That the

[14]Because of the assumed constancy of relative differences among industries in
income per gainfully occupied and because effects of inter-industry shifts are calculated as residuals, the measures in Table 14, line 10, include the effects of shifts
not only in the *shares* of industries in the total gainfully occupied but also in
relative inter-industry differences in income per gainfully occupied. The latter
element can be assumed to be minor.

relative effect of inter-industry shifts is greater during 1900-25 than during 1875-1900 may be due to the greater shift (shown in Table 12) during this later period away from agriculture toward the higher income per gainfully occupied industries (public utilities, finance, government).

The crude division into two periods reveals a distinct retardation in the rate of rise in income per gainfully occupied due to the intra- but not to the inter-industry component (lines 8 and 10). The increase in income per gainfully occupied due to intra-industry rises amounted in 1875-1900 to 40 percent of the 1875 base, and in 1900-25 to 21 percent of the 1900 base. Similar percentage rises associated with inter-industry shifts were 17 percent, 1875-1900, and 18 percent, 1900-25. While no retardation in the increase of income per gainfully occupied associated with the inter-industry component is observed, it is likely to appear as the shift toward the higher income per gainfully occupied industries slows down and approaches a limit.

3   Distribution by Type and Size

Long term changes in the distribution of income by type can be established for aggregate payments alone. And even in them, it is difficult to find marked trends, partly because the estimates that can be brought together for a sufficiently long period are none too comparable.

Bearing in mind the connection between the distribution of income by type and the character of business organization, one would expect that the secular decline in the relative weight of individual firms and the rise in the relative weight of corporations and of public institutions would mean a decline in the share of entrepreneurial income and possibly of rent, and a rise in the shares of employee compensation, dividends, and perhaps interest. One would be at a loss to form a similar hypothesis concerning the secular movement of the share of service income, on the one hand, i.e., of the sum of employee compensation and entrepreneurial income, and of property income, on the other.

The estimates confirm the hypothesis that can be formulated but with some qualifications (Table 15). The share of em-

TABLE 15

Aggregate Payments (Current Prices)

Percentage Distribution by Type, 1870-1938

		EMPLOYEE COMPEN- SATION (1)	ENTREP. NET INCOME (2)	SERVICE INCOME (3)	DIVI- DENDS (4)	INTER- EST (5)	RENT (6)	PROPERTY INCOME INCL. RENT (7)
		Based on King's Estimates of Value of Product						
	AVERAGE OF							
1	1870 & 1880	50.0	26.4	76.5		15.8	7.8	23.6
2	1880 & 1890	52.5	23.0	75.4		16.5	8.2	24.6
3	1890 & 1900	50.4	27.3	77.7		14.7	7.7	22.4
4	1900 & 1910	47.1	28.8	75.8		15.9	8.3	24.2
	Based on Martin's Estimates of Aggregate Payments excl. Entrepreneurial Savings							
	DECADE							
5	1899-08	59.5	23.8	83.3	5.3	5.1	6.4	16.7
6	1904-13	59.6	23.3	82.9	5.7	5.1	6.3	17.1
7	1909-18	59.7	23.3	83.0	6.5	4.9	5.7	17.0
8	1914-23	63.0	20.8	83.8	5.6	5.3	5.3	16.2
9	1919-28	65.1	18.3	83.4	5.4	6.0	5.2	16.6
	Based on NBER Estimates of Aggregate Payments incl. Entrepreneurial Savings							
	DECADE							
10	1919-28	61.7	19.5	81.2	5.6	6.1	7.1	18.8
11	1924-33	63.1	16.6	79.7	6.5	7.8	5.9	20.3
12	1929-38	64.9	15.9	80.8	6.6	8.4	4.3	19.2

LINE

1-4 W. I. King, *The Wealth and Income of the People of the United States* (Macmillan, 1919), Table **XXXI**, p. 160.

5-9 Based on estimates in *National Income in the United States, 1799-1938*, Tables 4, 41-4, and 46.

10-12 Based on estimates in *National Income and Its Composition*, Vol. One, Table 22.

ployee compensation does rise during the period as a whole: taking into consideration the differences among the various estimates, we may set it at below 60 percent of aggregate payments in the last quarter of the nineteenth century and well above it in the 1920's and the 1930's. But this rise is distinct only after World War I. The share of entrepreneurial income declined, but also not distinctly until after 1918. The two trends together leave the share of service income at a fairly constant level during the long period.

While the estimates for 1870-1910 combine dividends and interest, the relatively small role of industrial corporations around 1870 and their growth to importance by 1919 lead one to infer that the share of dividends must have risen appreciably. But since 1919 it seems to have risen little. The much greater rise in the share of interest is partly due to the relative inflexibility of interest during the severe depression of the 1930's. Yet it began immediately after World War I, reflecting the growth of government debt, which promises to produce a further rise in the future. The proportion accounted for by rent shows a downtrend, particularly marked in the recent depression decades.

One cannot feel too much confidence in the reliability and comparability of the estimates assembled in Table 15, particularly those for the earlier part of the period. The decade averages (lines 5-12), however, show consonance of whatever trends are observable—rise in the share of employee compensation, declines in those of entrepreneurial income and rent, recent rise in the interest share—with whatever expectations can be formed on the basis of other knowledge of changes in the type of business organization, growth in public debt, and the like. And it seems reasonable to conclude that there could hardly have been very great secular shifts in the relative distribution between service and property income, for if there had, they would probably find some reflection in the estimates, crude though the latter are.

We have not data adequate to establish the existence or absence of long term changes in the distribution of income payments among recipients grouped by size of their income. So far as the distribution by type has any effect on the distribution by size, one would infer from Table 15 that the relative inequality in the size distribution should show no marked secular changes. But the intra-type distribution of income by size is important in determining the characteristics of the distribution of income payments by size. The inequality in the distribution of employee compensation may have increased with the growth in the number of employees and with the inclusion of highly paid corporation executives and professional employees. The inequality in the distribution of entrepreneurial income may have increased also with the growth in the number of professional and other highly paid urban entrepreneurs. The only safe inference is that, given the relative secular constancy in the distribution of income payments by type, relative inequality in the size distribution of income, *so far as it was affected by shifts in the distribution by type;* cannot have undergone marked long term changes.

4 Distribution by Type of Use

One tends to assume that in earlier times, with greater pressure to build up the capital structure of the country, the share of current income devoted to capital formation was probably greater than it now is. In other words, one expects to find an uptrend in the share of the flow of goods to consumers and a downtrend in the share of net capital formation.

The estimates since 1869-78 confirm this expectation, but with significant qualifications (Table 16). First, the share of the flow of goods to consumers is consistently high: in no decade is it less than 80 percent of national income, and with two exceptions (in values in constant prices), not less than 85 percent. The predominance of ultimate consumption as the channel into which current product flows, noted for recent decades in Part I, is a characteristic of long standing in this country.[15]

Second, while the trend in the share of the flow of goods to consumers is upward and in the share of net capital formation downward, neither is pronounced unless we include the last two decades, which were affected by the 1929-32 depression and its aftermath. During the full period including the

[15]This moderate rate of capital formation may, at first glance, raise questions as to how the rapid growth of total product and of per capita, characterizing the period under study, was attained. In this connection, the importance of a high level of consumption as a base for increasing productivity, already mentioned in Part I, Section 5, should be borne in mind. In addition, two important factors, not directly reflected in the percentages net capital formation constitutes of national income, should be noted. First, through most of the period the country profited from large immigration. The capitalized value of this addition to the country's productive population was estimated to be more than $10 billion per year in the periods of largest immigration (1881-90 and 1901-14), and through the period 1860-1930 at roughly $6 to $7 billion per year, at prices of the 1920's (see calculation by Dr. Agostino de Vita, supplementing the article by Corrado Gini, Europa und Amerika: Zwei Welten, *Weltwirtschaftliches Archiv,* July 1940, v. 52, pp. 31-35). Second, through a substantial part of the period the country profited from availability of land for extensive expansion within its own boundaries.

TABLE 16

National Income, Percentage Distribution between
Flow of Goods to Consumers and Net Capital Formation, 1869-1938

	DECADE	CURRENT PRICES		1929 PRICES	
		Flow of Goods to Consumers (1)	Net Capital Formation (2)	Flow of Goods to Consumers (3)	Net Capital Formation (4)
1	1869-78	87.9	12.1	86.3	13.7
2	1874-83	87.0	13.0	85.6	14.4
3	1879-88	86.8	13.2	85.4	14.6
4	1884-93	85.9	14.1	83.9	16.1
5	1889-98	85.9	14.1	83.8	16.2
6	1894-03	86.4	13.6	85.2	14.8
7	1899-08	87.4	12.6	86.4	13.6
8	1904-13	87.9	12.1	86.9	13.1
9	1909-18	87.5	12.5	87.0	13.0
10	1914-23	87.6	12.4	88.6	11.4
11	1919-28	89.1	10.9	89.8	10.2
12	1924-33	93.3	6.7	94.0	6.0
13	1929-38	98.0	2.0	98.6	1.4
	Averages				
14	Lines 1-5	86.7	13.3	85.0	15.0
15	5-9	87.0	13.0	85.9	14.1
16	9-13	91.1	8.9	91.6	8.4
17	1-5	86.7	13.3	85.0	15.0
18	4-8	86.7	13.3	85.3	14.7
19	7-11	87.9	12.1	87.8	12.2

Calculated from estimates in *National Product since 1869*, Table II 16, col.
1, 3, 6, and 8.

latter, when the decades are grouped into three sets, each including five (with one overlapping), the share of the flow of goods to consumers (in constant prices) rises from 85 to 86 to 92 percent; the share of net capital formation declines from 15 to 14 to 8 percent, i.e., it is almost cut in half. If we exclude the last two decades, the decline in the share of capital formation is much less—from 15 percent in the early part of the period to somewhat over 12 percent in the last part. Also, this drop is rather minor, and the underlying estimates are not sufficiently precise to warrant confidence in such small changes. The decade estimates indicate that the decline was especially sharp after World War I, which suggests a connection with the upsurge in the flow of certain types of consumer goods whose supply was restricted during the war years. Setting aside the secular significance of the depression of the 1930's, we can say that if a long term decline in the proportion of net capital formation has occurred, it has been quite moderate so far.

The composition of the flow of goods to consumers and of net capital formation also shifted (Table 17). In the former, the main long term trend is the rise in the share of services not embodied in new commodities. In both groupings of decades, this share rose from 28 percent to one-third or more—an effect of both urbanization and the shift in demand toward services as the standard of living rose. There was also some tendency toward a rise in the share of consumer durable commodities—as part of the total flow of goods to consumers, and still more, of course, as part of the total flow of commodities to consumers. The shares of perishable and of semidurable commodities declined.

These secular changes in the composition of the flow of goods to consumers are not unexpected; indeed, they are a matter of common observation. That despite the length of the period covered, the rapid succession of technological changes, the sustained and cumulative growth of the supply of goods per consumer, the conspicuous shifts in consumers' tastes and modes of living, these secular changes, particularly in the percentage apportionment of commodity flow, were not greater is due largely to the fact that the various innovations tended to affect the several broad categories of commodities rather than only one. For example, the introduction and spread of passenger cars meant additions not only to consumer durable commodities but also to perishable (gasoline, oil), semidurable (tires), and services (repairs, garage service, etc.). Much greater shifts in the composition of consumer commodities could perhaps be observed if we had narrower categories. In the broad classification by durability in Table 17, the only marked secular change is in the apportionment between commodities and services.

The secular shifts in the composition of net capital formation are more pronounced (Table 17, lines 5-8). From 1869-78 to 1929-38 the shares of construction and of net additions to inventories declined: the former from over 70 percent in the first set of five decades to about 50 percent in the last set;

TABLE 17

Flow of Goods to Consumers and Net Capital Formation
Percentage Distribution by Type of Use, 1869-1938
(based on values in 1929 prices)

		A V E R A G E S O F D E C A D E S				
		Through 1938			Through 1928		
		1-5	5-9	9-13	1-5	4-8	7-11
		(1)	(2)	(3)	(4)	(5)	(6)
FLOW OF GOODS TO CONSUMERS (AVERAGES OF PERCENTAGES)							
1	Perishable	44.3	43.5	40.2	44.3	43.8	41.4
2	Semidurable	18.4	17.2	15.2	18.4	17.6	16.2
3	Durable	9.1	9.1	9.4	9.1	9.3	9.2
4	Services	28.2	30.3	35.2	28.2	29.3	33.2
	Total	100.0	100.0	100.0	100.0	100.0	100.0
NET CAPITAL FORMATION (PERCENTAGES OF AVERAGE VALUES)							
5	Producer durable	13.9	17.5	22.0	13.9	15.9	21.4
6	Construction	70.6	65.4	49.3	70.6	72.3	51.9
7	Net addition to inventories	18.3	13.7	12.1	18.3	13.4	15.6
8	Net changes in claims against foreign countries	—2.8	3.4	16.6	—2.8	—1.5	11.1
	Total	100.0	100.0	100.0	100.0	100.0	100.0

Calculated from estimates in *National Product since 1869*, Table II 8, col. 6-10, and Table II 15, col. 6-10. The decade numbers are those used in Table 16.

the latter, from 18 to 12 percent. The shares of producer durable equipment and net additions to claims against foreign countries rose: the former from 14 to 22 percent and the latter from a minus quantity to 17 percent of the total. Even if we exclude the last two decades as distorted by the depression of 1929-32, the secular trends in the composition of net capital formation away from construction and inventory accumulation and toward producer durable equipment and additions to claims against foreign countries are evident.

While the range of error in the estimates of various components of net capital formation is fairly wide, especially for the smaller items such as flow to inventories and additions to claims against foreign countries, the existence of these trends, if not their exact magnitude, can be asserted with confidence. As a country is industrialized, builds up its basic capital structure, and the growth in population retards, the share of construction in net capital formation (which includes all residential construction) declines. Likewise, as its distribution and transportation systems improve, and the proportion of seasonal industries (e.g., agriculture) declines, the share of

net additions to inventories also declines. As a country becomes an international creditor rather than a debtor, the
relative importance in net capital formation of additions to
claims against foreign countries rises; and as a large share
of capital investment goes into equipment and residential
construction plays a smaller role, the proportion of producer
durable equipment increases.

For the major components of net capital formation, construction, and producers' equipment, apportionment by broad
industrial categories of users can be estimated back to 1880.
The data for the years prior to the 1920's are the successive
wealth estimates, which have to be adjusted for both changes
in valuation and the inclusion of nonreproducible wealth, such
as land. They check only very roughly and over twenty-year
spans with cumulated totals of net capital formation derived
from data on commodity flow. Nevertheless, the orders of
magnitude indicated by the combination of these wealth and
capital formation data are sufficiently reliable to paint a broad
picture of changes in the industrial destination of net additions
to construction and equipment (Table 18).

In general, the share of private industries (agriculture, mining, manufacturing, etc., excluding public utilities and residential
construction), which was well over one-third during the first
twenty years, rose to 46 percent in the second twenty, then
declined to one-eighth of the total in the last twenty. The
share of public utilities remained fairly constant for the first
two periods—at about 30 and 26 percent—then rose to 37
percent in the third. That of residential construction declined
consistently, from 25 percent in the first twenty years to 17
percent in the last. The share of net construction and flow of
equipment under all private auspices has always been large,
but declined from 92 percent in the first twenty years to 91
percent in the second, and to 67 percent in the third. The
share of the tax exempt category, which includes government
and other activities under public auspices but is dominated by
the former, rose in the last twenty years to 33 percent of the
total, from below 10 percent during the preceding forty
years, indicating a definite upsurge in the share of public

TABLE 18
Industrial Distribution of Increase in Value of
Real Estate Improvements and Equipment, 1880-1939
(based on values in 1929 prices)

	June 1, 1880 to June 1, 1900 (1)	June 1, 1900 to Jan. 1, 1919 (2)	Jan. 1, 1919 to Jan. 1, 1939 (3)	June 1, 1880 to Jan. 1, 1939 (4)
% Share of Various Industrial Categories				
1 Private industry, excl. public utilities	36.1	46.1	12.5	34.0
2 Public utilities	30.4	26.0	37.2	30.4
3 Residential	25.4	19.1	16.9	20.8
4 Total private	91.9	91.3	66.6	85.2
5 Tax exempt	8.1	8.7	33.4	14.8
6 Total of above	100.0	100.0	100.0	100.0
% Share of Each Period within Industrial Category				
7 Private industry, excl. public utilities	37.7	53.0	9.3	100.0
8 Public utilities	35.5	33.5	31.0	100.0
9 Residential	43.4	36.0	20.6	100.0
10 Total private	38.3	41.9	19.8	100.0
11 Tax exempt	19.4	23.1	57.4	100.0
12 Total of above	35.5	39.1	25.4	100.0
% Rise in Durable Reproducible Wealth				
13 Private industry, excl. public utilities	166.2	97.2	8.2	441.4
14 Public utilities	172.2	65.4	34.6	484.7
15 Residential	183.5	58.9	20.0	422.9
16 Total private	172.7	76.3	19.3	451.0
17 Tax exempt	259.7	95.0	114.7	1,336.6
18 Total of above	177.5	77.6	26.8	499.9
19 Total wealth (line 18 + business inventories & claims against foreign countries)	169.8	92.9	32.4	557.6

LINE   COLUMN 1

1-12 Based on absolute totals in *National Product since 1869,* Table IV 13, Part B, col. 1.

13-18 Based on absolute totals in *ibid.,* Table IV 12, Part 8, col. 1 and 3.

19 Based on absolute totals in *ibid.,* Table IV 10, col. 6, lines 1 and 3.

COLUMN 2

1-12 Derived from *ibid.,* Table IV 13, Part B, col. 2.

13-18 Derived from *ibid.,* Table IV 12, Part B, col. 3, and Table IV 7, col. 3 and 6. The rates were adjusted to a 20-year basis to establish comparability with those in col. 1 and 3.

19 Derived from the totals underlying line 18 plus *ibid.,* Table IV 10, line 3, col. 3 and 4, for 1900, and line 10, col. 3 and 4, for 1919. The rate was adjusted to a 20-year basis.

COLUMN 3

1-12 Derived from *ibid.,* Table IV 13, Part B, col. 4.

13-18 Derived from *ibid.* and Table IV 12, Part B, col. 6.

19 Additions to totals underlying line 18 from *ibid.,* Table IV 10, lines 10 and 12.

COLUMN 4

See notes to col. 1-3.

construction and equipment during the two decades following World War I. The total increase in value for all sixty years (col. 4) is distributed about one-third to private industry (excluding public utilities and residential construction); about three-tenths to public utilities; about one-fifth to residential construction; and about one-seventh to activities under public auspices.

These differences in the shares of the broad industrial categories of users among the three periods mean differences also in the shares contributed during each period to the total for the sixty years. Of total net construction and equipment added to private industry (excluding public utilities and residential construction) the first period contributed 38 percent; the second, though somewhat shorter, 53 percent; and the third, only slightly over 9 percent. For public utilities, there was a consistent though moderate decline in the contribution of each period. Of the total added to residential construction, the share of the first period was about 43 percent; of the second, 36 percent; of the third, only 21 percent. Of the total added to construction and equipment under public auspices, on the contrary, considerably less than one-half was added during the first forty years, and 57 percent during the last twenty, 1919-38.

The minor secular decline in the share of net capital formation in national income, indicated by Table 16, would be bigger were we to measure only the share of net capital formation under *private* auspices. While the estimates in Table 18 do not cover net additions to inventories and to claims against foreign countries, they do cover the two components that account on the average for more than three-quarters of net capital formation—construction and producers' equipment— and they show a marked decline in the share of private construction and equipment.

The fact that of the total sixty years' accumulation more than one-third was added during the first twenty and much less than one-third during the last twenty (Table 18, line 12) suggests a retardation in the rate of growth of *durable reproducible* wealth (i.e., net stock of construction and equipment). Such retardation can be measured, since the total stock in 1880 was calculated for the purpose of estimating net additions between 1880 and 1919 (Table 18, lines 13-19).

For both total durable reproducible wealth and every category distinguished, the stock increased at a sharply declining rate. While that in private industry (excluding public utilities and residential construction) more than quintupled during the sixty years, the percentage increase in the first twenty was 166 and in the last twenty 8. The declines in the percentage rate of growth are equally drastic in other categories; and even in the tax exempt group, the large addition in the last twenty years, 115 percent, is smaller than in the first twenty, 260 percent. For the total of the categories distinguished (line 18), which sextuples, the percentage rate of increase drops from 178 in the first twenty years to 27 in the last twenty.

The estimates may well exaggerate the degree of retardation in the rate of increase in the stock of durable reproducible capital, largely because the initial estimate for 1880 may be too low and the last twenty years include the unusually severe depression of the 1930's. Yet, the decline in the percentage rate of accumulation is shown even if we exclude the last twenty years. Also, even if we add the two missing components of total reproducible wealth which can be estimated (although not by industrial affiliation of holder or user)—business inventories and the balance of claims against foreign countries—the total (line 19) still exhibits a declining percentage rate of growth, even though the retardation is not as marked as in the narrower total limited to real estate improvements and durable equipment.

A decline in the rate of relative additions to durable reproducible capital does not necessarily mean a decline in the rate of increase in the productive services such capital can contribute. The price and value indexes available to translate construction and equipment in changing values to a constant price or value base do not take adequate account of the improved efficiency of capital. Yet it cannot be assumed that such unreflected improvement in efficiency was enough greater during the last part of the sixty years to offset the retardation in the rate of relative additions to the stock. Indeed, one might argue that it may well have been relatively greater between 1880 and 1900 than between 1919 and 1939. But we do not have definite evidence on the subject; all one can say about the figures in Table 18 is that the total stock of capital in the country available for the production process grew at a high rate during the sixty years and the rate declined sharply from the early to the later part of the period.

This conclusion, together with the retardation in the rate of increase in the other important productive factor, viz., labor supply as represented by the gainfully occupied, noted in Section 2, helps to explain the retardation in the rate of growth of national income. Furthermore, the reduction in the average rate of utilization of the labor supply, as represented by fewer working hours, and the greater retardation in the rate of growth of reproducible capital than in the labor supply[16] at least suggest why the rate of increase in income per gainfully occupied (disregarding unemployment) should also have declined. The subject, obviously of telling importance, awaits further exploration—not only in this but also in countries that entered the phase of modern industrialization earlier or later.

5 Fluctuations in Rates of Growth

The percentage changes from decade to decade in Table 10 (col. 4-6) show marked fluctuations which in their recurrence have the appearance of cycles. Thus, the entries for national income (col. 4) drop from the large increase in the average for 1874-83 over that for 1869-78 to a much smaller increase in the average for 1889-98 over that for 1884-93; then the rates of change rise again, only to decline after one or two intervals. Inspection of Table 10 reveals the existence of at least three such swings in the rate of growth with a

[16]Compare the movement of rates in Table 18, lines 18 and 19, with that of total population (Table 10, col. 5, lines 15-20) or the gainfully occupied (Table 14, line 2).

span from trough to trough of four to five entries, representing periods of twenty to twenty-five years.

While the causes of such fluctuations in the rate of secular growth are still obscure and their recurrence not too widely known, sufficient study has been made to affirm their existence.[17] It may be of interest to establish here their characteristics as revealed by the comprehensive decade estimates at our disposal. The fact that these estimates are decade averages makes it impossible to study the fluctuations with as much precision as might be desired. Yet, for swings so long in duration, even decade estimates, overlapping by five years, suffice to establish the broad characteristics of timing and amplitude.

In order to bring out these characteristics clearly, the longer term trend—the downward drift—of the rates of change from decade to decade must be eliminated. Two procedures were employed for this purpose. First, a straight line was fitted to all the series, by the method of least squares, to the logarithms of the rates of change between overlapping

[17]In *Measuring Business Cycles* (National Bureau of Economic Research, 1946, Ch. 11), Burns and Mitchell analyze the various hypotheses of long cycles, testing their validity in terms of differences in characteristics of specific short cycles between those in the rising and in the declining long phases of the presumptive long swings. With few exceptions, no significant differences are revealed; so that one may question whether the observed long cycles are not due merely to the averaging out of some of the more conspicuous, irregular peculiarities of the shorter term fluctuations observed in various aspects of economic activity.

This, however, does not justify the dismissal of these changes in the rate of secular growth from study. That these long term swings may be nought but averages of short cycles, in which some of the larger, irregular peculiarities of the latter are 'stretched out' over longer periods is no more reason to dismiss them than we can dismiss the shorter cycles themselves because they can be interpreted as results of averaging of changes essentially random in character. (See the author's article on Random Events and Cyclical Oscillations, *Journal of the American Statistical Association*, Sept. 1929, pp. 258-75.) These swings in rate of secular movement represent a component of the time series that is omitted from view if we confine our attention to the average rate of growth and the average retardation in it, on the one hand; and to changes in the series within the short term cycles (either specific or reference), on the other. Analysis of this component seems definitely worth while, so long as we do not assign to these fluctuations in the secular rate of growth the character of cycles, since their periodic recurrence has not yet been demonstrated or explained.

decades. This line was found to provide a good fit in most
series. But the few exceptions forced the adoption of a
second procedure—marking off the troughs of the successive
long swings; assembling the single rates of change into three
groups in accordance with the dates of the long swings; calculating means of the logarithms of these groups of rates;
and using these means as three points to calculate the constants and ordinates of a second degree potential curve fitted
to the logarithms. In most series, this procedure yielded
results not much different from the straight line; and the latter was retained. In a few, the three point curve provided a
significantly better fit; and hence served to establish more
reliably the characteristics of the long swings.

Deviations from the straight line or from the three point
curve provide then a description of the alterations in the
rate of growth, free from the effect of both the average level
of such rates and from the downward trend in them. They
are shown for national income, population, and per capita
income in Table 19. In addition, the table provides certain
over-all measures—the average rate of growth and of its
retardation,[18] as well as the average deviation—a rough measure of the amplitude of swings in the rates of growth.

The measures of retardation in Tables 19-21 reflect the
common tendency of the rates of growth to decline—a tendency already discussed in Section 1. They indicate the percentage
by which the underlying rate of increase declines with the pas-
sage of each quinquennium. Thus, for national income the
average rate of retardation is 2.2 percent; that is, in every
quinquennium the trend rate of increase is reduced by that
percentage (e.g., for the interval between 1874-83 and 1869-
78 the trend rate of increase; i.e., the ordinate of the straight
line, is 34.3 percent; for the next interval, 1879-88 to 1874-

[18] These measures are antilogs of the two constants of the equation of the straight
line fitted to rates of change between overlapping decades. The average rate of
change is the antilog of the constant a and the average rate of retardation is the
antilog of the constant b, in the equation $\log y = a + bx$, in which y is the rate
of change and x is in units of quinquennia. Throughout, the origin of x was taken
as the midpoint of the full period covered by the series.

TABLE 19
Fluctuations in Rates of Growth, National Income
Total and Per Capita (1929 Prices), 1869-1938

CENTRAL YEAR OF PERIOD (1)	PERCENTAGE DEVIATIONS FROM STRAIGHT LINE OR 3 POINT CURVE FITTED TO RATES OF PERCENTAGE CHANGE BETWEEN OVERLAPPING DECADES			STANDARD TREND-CYCLE	
	National Income (2)	Population* (3)	Per Capita (4)	Central Year of Period (5)	Trend-cycle of Quinquennial Rates (6)
1 1876	+8.5	+0.5	+8.7	1875	—2.0
2 1881	+0.1	+0.5	+0.3	1880	+7.2
3 1886	—8.3	+0.3	—8.3	1885	—3.0
4 1891	—8.4	—0.4	—8.3	1890	—7.7
5 1896	+0.4	—0.7	+1.0	1895	—5.4
6 1901	+4.6	—0.3	+4.4	1900	+12.6
7 1906	+2.8	+0.4	+1.9	1905	+1.0
8 1911	—1.9	+0.2	—2.7	1910	—0.5
9 1916	+1.1	—0.6	+1.5	1915	+3.0
10 1921	+10.1	+0.3	+9.5	1920	—7.7
11 1926	—0.9	+0.6	—1.4	1925	+1.5
12 1931	—6.1	—0.7	·—4.8		

Summary Measures, 1869-1938
13 Av. % rate of growth per quinquennium	+18.6	+9.3	+8.5		
14 Av. % rate of retardation per quinquennium	—2.2	—0.6	—1.7		
15 Av. % deviation (geometric mean)	4.5	0.5	4.5		4.8

*Deviations from a 3 point curve; columns 2, 4, and 6, deviations from a straight line.

COLUMN

2-4 Calculated from estimates in Table 10 by methods described in the text.
5 & 6 From Arthur F. Burns, *Production Trends in the United States since 1870* (National Bureau of Economic Research, 1934), Ch. V and Table 53, p. 324: Burns' trend-cycles for annual rates of growth have been recalculated to quinquennial rates by raising them to the fifth power.

83, it is 31.3 percent. The decline is 3.0 percent or 2.2 per⁻ cent of 134.3.)

The main interest of Table 19 is, however, in the characteristics of the long swings in rates of growth. Centering the intervals for which these rates are measured, we can observe the approximate timing of the swings. National income, population, and income per capita each have about three swings, although the first and the last may be incompletely covered. From an apparent peak in the interval centering on 1876, the rate of change in national income and in income per capita declines to a trough in the interval centering on 1891; rises to another peak in the interval centering on 1901; declines to another trough in the interval centering on 1911; rises to the last observable peak in the interval centering on 1921; and drops to the last observable trough in the interval centering on 1931. The average period between troughs is twenty years; that between peaks, 22.5 years.

The average duration of these swings indicates similarity to the secondary secular movements established in the author's *Secular Movements in Production and Prices* (Houghton Mifflin, 1930, Ch. IV) and to the trend-cycles as measured by Arthur F. Burns in his *Production Trends in the United States since 1870* (National Bureau of Economic Research, 1934, Ch. V). Because the procedures used here are similar to Burns', it is of interest to compare the deviations in columns 2 and 4 with the trend-cycles as established by Burns on the basis of various production series for a large number of industries. The entries in column 6 constitute Burns' 'standard trend-cycle', i.e., medians of the deviations of rates of growth within successive decades from a straight line fitted to such rates over the full period he covers. The only modification was to recalculate these deviations so that they applied to quinquennial rather than to annual rates of change.

The comparison shows fair conformity of fluctuations derived for national income, total and per capita (col. 2 and 4), with those derived from a variety of indexes of physical volume of output (col. 6). There is a minor disparity in the first swing, Burns' series showing a low entry about 1875 and our series a high entry about 1876. The agreement then persists up to the last two entries that can be compared in the two series. There is some reason to suppose that the entry for the interval centering on 1925 is too high in the Burns series, based as it was upon incomplete coverage of the 1929-32 depression (most series used by Burns ended in 1930). Also, the differences for the two postwar intervals, those centering on 1875-76 and 1920-21, may be due partly to different timing of the periods covered; partly to the more comprehensive coverage of national income, with its fuller reflection of the wartime decline in civilian production and its greater postwar recovery. In any collection of annual production series, even as comprehensive as that assembled and analyzed by Burns, highly fabricated consumer products and services not embodied in commodities tend to be neglected.[19]

But even taking the discrepancies as they stand, the agreement between the two series is close enough to warrant the conclusion that they support each other in affirming the existence of long swings in the rates of growth, and of their rough duration and timing for the period covered by both studies. Another indirect but significant indication that such swings are not a figment of statistical imagination is their presence in the population series (Table 19, col. 3). In view of the substantial independence of population and national income estimates,[20] it is significant that population also reveals swings in the rate of growth of duration and timing not too dissimilar to those in national income.

[19]The present series and those used by Burns are not completely independent. In deriving the annual estimates for 1869-88 (converted later to overlapping decade averages), we used, for interpolation between the Census year values, many of the series analyzed by Burns (see *National Product since 1869*, Part II). Shaw's annual series, which begin with 1889, are interpolations between Census dates based largely upon state data; but even they are dependent in part upon annual production series used as supplementary bases of interpolation—particularly for 1889-99 (see W. H. Shaw, *Value of Commodity Output since 1869*, National Bureau of Economic Research, in press, particularly Table II 6). Nevertheless, the use of Census data for the base years, and of state data for annual interpolation for the period since 1889, as well as the wider coverage of our series, mean that the latter are largely independent of the data Burns used. Conformity, or lack of conformity, between the fluctuations in the rate of change shown by our estimates and Burns' standard trend-cycle can, therefore, be deemed significant.

[20]Population and related figures on the gainfully occupied are used in the annual estimates of national income since 1919 to check the coverage of the industry by industry subtotals; and for the decade series for the period before 1919 primarily to estimate construction, for decades before 1870 (as the basis for the allowance for depreciation in the period since 1869). In both uses, the quantitative effect of population data on national income estimates is so minor that the two series may be treated as virtually independent.

However, these fluctuations in the rate of growth of population are much narrower in amplitude than those in the rate of growth of national income, total or per capita. Part of the difference may be due to defects of annual population estimates, which, for lack of basic data, do not reflect true annual change sensitively. But part of the difference is undoubtedly genuine, population not responding as readily to whatever factors produce these swings in the rate of growth of both it and national income. Another significant difference is in the timing of the long swings: while the timing pattern in national income and population is fairly similar, the swings in the latter lag behind those in the former. The troughs and peaks in the population rates of growth lag fairly consistently by one interval behind those in the rates of growth of national income. This suggests that whatever the contribution of fluctuations in the rate of change of population to those in the rate of change of national income, the former are more in the nature of a delayed effect of whatever factors produce the swings in the rate of change of national income.

We now turn to fluctuations in the rate of change in the flow of goods to consumers and its components (Table 20). With respect to the timing of these fluctuations, there is substantial similarity between the flow of goods to consumers and national income (col. 6 and 7)—not surprising in view of the preponderant proportion the former constitutes of the latter. Nor is it surprising to find the swings in the rate of change in the volume of services similar to those in the flow of goods to consumers—since the decade estimates for services were derived by applying gradually rising sample ratios to total consumer commodities. But it is significant that the swings in the rates of change in the three groups of consumer commodities are similar—since the estimates for perishable, semidurable, and durable commodities were each derived independently. Apparently whatever factors tend to produce these swings affect the flow of the major categories of consumer commodities at roughly the same time.

While the timing is similar, the amplitude of the swings is not. That in the rates of change in perishable and semi-

TABLE 20

Fluctuations in Rates of Growth, Flow of Goods to Consumers and Its Components (1929 Prices), 1869-1938

PERCENTAGE DEVIATIONS FROM STRAIGHT LINE OR 3 POINT CURVE FITTED
TO RATES OF PERCENTAGE CHANGE BETWEEN OVERLAPPING DECADES

	CENTRAL YEAR OF PERIOD (1)	Perish-able* (2)	Semidurable (3)	Durable (4)	Services (5)	Flow of Goods to Consumers (6)	National Income (7)
1	1876	+10.5	+5.4	+3.2	+6.1	+9.2	+8.5
2	1881	—0.2	+1.3	+5.6	—1.3	+0.7	+0.1
3	1886	—11.1	—6.1	—2.8	—10.0	—9.4	—8.3
4	1891	—6.1	—7.9	—11.1	—9.3	—8.6	—8.4
5	1896	+5.3	—0.1	—4.1	+3.4	+1.7	+0.4
6	1901	+6.0	+5.7	+0.3	+9.9	+5.2	+4.6
7	1906	+2.2	+3.3	—0.8	+5.8	+2.0	+2.8
8	1911	—2.4	—1.7	—1.7	—4.3	—3.7	—1.9
9	1916	—1.8	—2.6	+7.1	+4.7	+0.7	+1.1
10	1921	+3.4	+6.8	+28.2	+9.4	+8.7	+10.1
11	1926	—1.9	+4.7	—0.8	—1.5	+0.5	—0.9
12	1931	—2.1	—7.2	—16.9	—9.9	—5.1	—6.1

Summary Measures, 1869-1938

13	Av. % rate of growth per quinquennium	+19.5	+16.8	+19.9	+22.0	+19.9	+18.6
14	Av. % rate of retardation per quinquennium	—1.9	—2.0	—2.4	—1.4	—1.8	—2.2
15	Av. % deviation (geometric mean)	4.5	4.5	7.0	6.6	4.7	4.5

*Deviations from a 3 point curve; all other columns, deviations from a straight line.

COLUMN

2-6 Calculated from estimates in *National Product since 1869,* Table II 8, col. 6-10.
  7 Table 19, col. 2.

durable commodities is distinctly narrower than in durable or in services (line 15).[21] The reasons are not easily suggested. But it is interesting to note that the wider amplitude in durable commodities is due largely to the difference for the last observable swing (lines 8-12) comprising the intervals centered on 1911, 1916, 1921, 1926, and 1931; whereas the wider amplitude for services is observable in the last two swings. The general sensitiveness of consumer durable goods to fluctuations in economic conditions, particularly during

[21]The use of the three point curve for the perishable group does not affect the comparison, since the average deviation from the straight line is only slightly larger (4.7 instead of 4.5).

recent decades when they comprised more semi-luxuries than in earlier times, is readily admitted. And perhaps there is a similar element of semi-luxury demand in the services category, especially since the extension and intensification of the urban style of living.

While the long swings in the rate of change in the flow of goods to consumers and in its components are similar with respect to timing and not too different in amplitude from those in national income, distinctly different characteristics emerge for net capital formation and the two of its components for which analysis in terms of percentage changes is possible (Table 21). For the producer durable category, the timing of the swings in the rate of change is closely similar to that in national income and in the flow of goods to consumers. But the amplitude is much wider, the geometric mean deviation being over 25 percent as compared with less than 5 percent for national income and the flow of goods to consumers; and this despite the use of the three point curve which in this case, unlike others, yields a much smaller average deviation than a straight line. To a considerable extent, however, this wider amplitude is due to the fact that the flow of producer durables is measured *net,* and fluctuations in its rate of change compared with the *gross* flow of goods to consumers. Yet even for gross producer durables, the average deviation from the three point curve is 7.5 percent—greater than for any component analyzed so far.[22]

Fluctuations in the rate of change of construction are of still wider amplitude; and even when taken gross, the volume of construction is subject to rates of change whose fluctuations average more than 12 percent. Equally significant is the different timing of swings in the rate of change in construction:

[22]Arthur F. Burns has found a related difference in the amplitude of 'trend-cycles' between consumer goods ("products destined for human consumption") and producer goods ("products which find final realization in industrial equipment"). For 29 consumer goods series both the median and arithmetic mean of trend-cycle amplitudes were 1.6 percent (in terms of *annual* rates of growth); for 14 producer goods series the median of trend-cycle amplitudes was 2.4 percent, the arithmetic mean, 2.6 percent (see *Production Trends in the United States since 1870,* note 44, p. 229).

TABLE 21

Fluctuations in Rates of Growth

Net Capital Formation and Its Components (1929 Prices), 1869-1938

	CENTRAL YEAR OF PERIOD (1)	Net Producer Durable* (2)	Net Construc- tion (3)	Net Capital Formation* (4)	National Income (5)	Building Permits (6)	Popu- lation* (7)
		PERCENTAGE DEVIATIONS FROM STRAIGHT LINE OR 3 POINT CURVE FITTED TO RATES OF PERCENTAGE CHANGE BETWEEN OVERLAPPING DECADES					
1	1876	+60.1	—20.6	+30.9	+8.5	—13.2	+0.5
2	1881	+4.9	—1.9	+6.4	+0.1	+14.3	+0.5
3	1886	—27.7	+11.1	—2.0	—8.3	+10.6	+0.3
4	1891	—33.4	—6.1	—13.4	—8.4	—11.5	—0.4
5	1896	+7.4	—15.2	—14.7	+0.4	—18.3	—0.7
6	1901	+29.7	+12.5	—7.6	+4.6	+6.8	—0.3
7	1906	—12.8	+23.9	+1.6	+2.8	+8.5	+0.4
8	1911	+6.7	—5.3	+10.4	—1.9	—16.8	+0.2
9	1916	+17.1	—16.2	+14.0	+1.1	+12.0	—0.6
10	1921	+31.7	+159.1	+48.0	+10.1	+88.3	+0.3
11	1926	—17.1	+66.0	+7.0	—0.9	+3.5	+0.6
12	1931	—25.5	—69.5	—47.0	—6.1	—40.1	—0.7

Summary Measures, 1869-1938

13	Av. % rate of growth per quinquennium	+3.3	—2.5	—1.7	+18.6	+11.7	+9.3
14	Av. % rate of retardation per quinquennium	—8.3	—10.1	—9.7	—2.2	—5.4	—0.6
15	Av. % devia- tion (geometric mean)	25.2	37.1	18.9	4.5	21.4	0.5

*Deviations from a 3 point curve; columns 3, 5, and 6, deviations from a straight line.

COLUMN

2-4 Calculated from estimates in *National Product since 1869,* Table II 15, col. 6-10.

5 & 7 Table 19, col. 2 and 3.

6 Calculated from estimates given for 1874-1929 in Arthur F. Burns, *Production Trends in the United States since 1870,* pp. 302-303, and extrapolated from 1929 on the basis of an index derived by dividing the permit valuation of building operations (*Statistical Abstract, 1942,* Table 960, p. 990) by a cost of construction index calculated from estimates in *National Product since 1869,* Tables I 7 and I 8, col. 8. The 1869-78 decade was extrapolated on the basis of changes in gross construction, with a rough allowance for the wider amplitude of decade to decade changes in the building permits series.

the first two swings lag substantially behind those in national income or the flow of producer durables, the third alone is synchronous with that in national income and its other major components. That both the wider amplitude and different timing are characteristic of long term swings in the rate of change in construction is confirmed by the series on building permits (col. 6). The latter, reflecting the *gross* volume of construction, shows an average deviation of more than 21 percent, and swings of a timing closely similar to that for net construction in column 3.[23]

The coincidence between the swings in the rate of change in construction and those in population (col. 3 and 7) is of interest: in the last two swings, the peaks and troughs in the rate of change in construction and in population are synchronous except for the peak in the last, and even in the first swing construction, like population, reaches a peak later than the rate of change in national income and its other components. There is thus a definite suggestion that changes in the rate of growth of population affect those in the rate of growth of construction, presumably through the influence of the former primarily on residential construction and types closely related to it (commercial, some of the public utility, educational, etc.).

Because of the lack of synchronism between the swings in the rates of change in producer durable commodities and in construction, and the importance of these two components in net capital formation, the swings in the rate of change in the latter are a hybrid dissimilar to those in either component or in national income (col. 4). Indeed, as a result of the cancellation of divergent fluctuations in the components, two rather than three distinct swings are observed in the rate of change in net capital formation. The amplitude of the swings, though narrower than in either producer durables or

[23]The lack of synchronism in timing between the long swings in construction and those in comprehensive measures of production at large is also confirmed by Burns' findings. His measures of conformity to the standard trend-cycle pattern, which measure the degree of similarity in timing between the trend-cycles of any given series and that of the general pattern of all industries, are fairly low for construction. Of nine series classified as relating to construction (see *ibid.,* Chart 18, p. 222, and Tables 35 and 36, pp. 216-19), the most important—building permits—has an index of conformity of —0.11; two others (gypsum and white lead) have indexes below 0; one (flaxseed consumption), an index of 0; of the remaining series the two relating to rails each have indexes of 0.60; two (nails and total cement), indexes of 0.50; and one (roofing slate), an index of 0.37. The low conformity, particularly of series closely related to residential construction, is conspicuous.

construction, remains wide; and even on a gross basis it averages 6.0 percent, wider than in the flow of goods to consumers or in national income.

The analysis of fluctuations in the rates of growth must perforce be confined here to national product and its major components by type of use; and has to be pursued much further before sufficient light is shed upon this particular type of change in the rate of growth of the economy. They have been discussed here at some length because of their importance in using the long term trends of the past as a basis for judging the future. Obviously, the existence of these long swings in the rate of secular movement must always be borne in mind in trying to interpret economic changes observed over a few decades; and they render particularly difficult judgments of prospective secular levels based upon observations confined to two or three decades of an immediate past.

In addition, the analysis suggests conclusions relevant to a proper interpretation of the fluctuations of the 1920's and 1930's. Tables 19-21 indicate that these recent decades witnessed a coincidence of the long swings in the rates of secular change in all the components of national income, including construction, whereas during the earlier decades swings in the rate of change in construction followed a timing pattern different from that in the flow of goods to consumers and in producer durable commodities. Whether this circumstance serves to explain the special severity of economic fluctuations in the recent two decades is a question that cannot be answered definitively here. But this conclusion from the analysis just presented may help in understanding the events of the last two decades, and in forming a proper judgment of their secular significance.

PART III

Changes during Business Cycles, 1900—1938

The economy's behavior during business cycles is not revealed sharply by the available estimates of national income and its components, for they cover a short period; being annual rather than monthly, they fail to show timing and amplitude precisely; and the margin of error is fairly wide, especially for some components. Yet national income series are the most comprehensive measures of the economy; and differences among various sectors in their behavior during business cycles can be observed better in its components than in other bodies of data.

Because of this unique advantage, we summarize what national income estimates show concerning changes during periods commonly recognized as defining cycles in the economy at large, called 'reference' cycles. Series for such wide time units as years afford little opportunity to establish differences in timing. And there is little need for studying 'specific' cycles, i.e., cycles in individual series, as by and large and for obvious reasons, the short term fluctuations in national income and in most of its components take place within reference cycles. Consequently, the summary is confined to changes during reference cycles, and attention is centered on the consistency and magnitude of the changes.

1 *The Magnitude of Changes*

Before we consider the differences in the degree to which national income and its components fluctuate during business cycles, we try to give some notion of the absolute magnitude of the changes (Table 22).

During each reference expansion, national income and employment rose substantially; during each reference contraction,

73

TABLE 22

National Income (1929 Prices) and Aggregate Employment
Changes during Reference Cycles, 1919-1938

| | | NATIONAL INCOME (billions of dollars) | | AGGREGATE EMPLOYMENT (Employees & Entrepreneurs—millions) | |
		Total Change (1)	Change per Year (2)	Total Change (3)	Change per Year (4)
	Cycle 1919-21				
1	Change, 1919-20	+1.5	+1.5	+0.4	+0.4
2	Change, 1920-21	—3.3	—3.3	—3.7	—3.7
3	Difference		—4.8		—4.1
	Cycle 1921-24				
4	Change, 1921-23	+14.0	+7.0	+4.3	+2.2
5	Change, 1923-24	+1.3	+1.3	—0.2	—0.2
6	Difference		—5.7		—2.3
	Cycle 1924-27				
7	Change, 1924-26	+7.3	+3.6	+2.1	+1.1
8	Change, 1926-27	+0.9	+0.9	+0.1	+0.1
9	Difference		—2.7		—1.0
	Cycle 1927-32				
10	Change, 1927-29	+7.0	+3.5	+2.0	+1.0
11	Change, 1929-32	—31.4	—10.5	—8.9	—3.0
12	Difference		—13.9		—4.0
	Cycle 1932-38				
13	Change, 1932-37	+28.5	+5.7	+7.8	+1.6
14	Change, 1937-38	—3.3	—3.3	—2.4	—2.4
15	Difference		—9.0		—4.0
	Average for 5 Cycles				
16	Change, expansion	+11.6	+4.3	+3.3	+1.2
17	Change, contraction	—7.1	—3.0	—3.0	—1.8
18	Difference		—7.2		—3.1

COLUMN
1 Based on estimates in *National Product since 1869,* Table I 19, col. 3.
3 Based on estimates in *National Income and Its Composition,* Vol. One, Table 8.

both either declined or rose at rates materially lower than
during the preceding or following expansion; during each
reference cycle the rate of change declined sharply from expansion to contraction. The rise in national income averaged
close to $12 billion (in 1929 prices) for the five reference
expansions, or somewhat over $4 billion per year; the decline
averaged somewhat more than $7 billion for the five reference
contractions, or $3 billion per year. The increase in employ-
ment averaged for the five reference expansions 3.3 million,
or 1.2 million per year; and the decline was 3 million, or 1.8
million per year.

The consistency of the marked alterations in the rate of movement in national income and employment from reference expansion to contraction is hardly surprising. The reference dates were fixed in terms of cycles in general business activity; and comprehensive measures of output and employment should vary in close agreement with such a reference chronology. If the estimates of national income and employment are fairly accurate, any lack of consonance between short term fluctuations in them and the reference cycle chronology would be reason for questioning the validity of the latter, not a symptom of any substantive problem calling for investigation.[24]

The interesting points about the estimates in Table 22 are the substantial changes during reference cycles and the frequency of either absolute declines or of sharp drops in the rate of increase. During the two decades national income in 1929 prices averaged $70.5 billion; employment averaged 40.5 million; and the average decline per depression year in both was more than 4 percent of the average level. Of the 19 year-to-year changes in the two decades, there were five large absolute declines in national income; in three other years the increase dwindled to relatively negligible proportions. The same was essentially true of employment, there being five years of large absolute declines, one year of small absolute decline, and three years in which the increase was relatively inappreciable. In other words, substantial rises characterized at most 11 year-to-year changes out of 19.

This very fluctuation in the short term rate of output and employment constitutes a problem, even if we disregard any effect on the average level for the longer period. Ignoring for the moment a possible lowering of the *secular* level of output and employment due to the loss of opportunities during depressions, we assume that the average level attained during the

[24]The upturns and downturns (the latter allowing for breaks in the rate of change) of the annual series for both national income (in 1929 prices) and total employment are identical in timing with the annual chronology of reference cycles and phases established by the Business Cycle Study of the National Bureau of Economic Research. Since neither series was available at the time the chronology was established, the conformity constitutes a corroboration of it.

twenty years would have been conducive to greater welfare had it materialized at either equal or steadily rising rates each year. Final users, ultimate consumers or purchasers of net additions to the stock of capital, would have enjoyed greater returns had consumer and capital goods remained constant or risen steadily. This particular aspect of the business cycle problem cannot be analyzed here.

We can attempt, however, an illustrative calculation of the second aspect mentioned just above. The question is: what would have been the secular movement of national income had the economy not been plagued by conspicuous cyclical depressions? If we can estimate this potential secular movement at all, we can approximate the loss due to cyclical contractions.

One way of answering the question would be to assume that increases attained during the cyclical expansions measured the economy's long term capacity. The reasoning would be somewhat as follows. Had there been no cyclical contractions, the long term growth would have been much greater. Undisturbed by cyclical contractions, the economy would increase its output at the rate it attained during cyclical expansions. Applying the annual rate of increase in national income during cyclical expansions in Table 22, $4.3 billion, to the period covered in the table, we calculate that national income would have grown $81.7 billion; or from $58.2 in 1919 (our estimate of national income in 1929 prices) to $139.9 billion in 1938. As national income in 1938 was $80.7 billion, the loss for this year alone was $59.2 billion, or almost 75 percent of the level actually attained. For each year in the period we could compare the hypothetical level, calculated by adding $4.3 billion per year to the level for 1919, with the actual income realized, and derive the deficit or excess.

The fallacy in this crude calculation is the identification of rates during cyclical expansions with the possible secular rate. The very depth to which the economy sinks during a depression is a factor in the rise during the succeeding expansion; and the rapidity with which output can increase from the trough of a cycle, permitted by existing productive capacity and stimulated by accumulated deficits in purchases by ultimate consumers or users of capital goods, is no indication of the steady rate at which it would grow during a long period. The average in Table 22, line 16, column 2, being partly inflated by years of rebound from sharp contractions, is likely to be altogether too high as a rate for sustained secular growth. This conclusion is confirmed when we apply a similar calculation to employment. Its average annual rate of growth during cyclical expansions, 1.2 million, applied to the period yields a total increase in employment from 1919 to 1938 of 22.8 million; which, added to the estimated employment in 1919, 39.8 million, would mean employment of 62.6 million in 1938. Yet the total gainfully occupied in that year was about 55 million.[25] And allowing for minimum frictional unemployment, it is difficult to see how employment could much exceed 52 million.

A more valid approach to the problem is set forth in Table 23, although even here the results are merely illustrative. We have data on the number of the gainfully occupied during the period. This being the most important productive resource, its secular increase is certainly one factor contributing to the secular rise in national income. The other is the rise in income per employed, due partly to the increasing efficiency of the worker himself, partly to the increased supply of capital per worker. To calculate this second factor, we compared national income in constant prices per *employed* (i.e., entrepreneurs and employed wage earners and salaried workers) at the beginning and end of the twenty years, averaging 1919 with 1920 and 1937 with 1938 to eliminate the effects of cyclical changes without canceling too much of the secular rise itself. Prorating per year this total increase in income per employed yielded column 2. Combining the two factors making for the

[25]This figure is quoted from *National Income and Its Composition*, Vol. One, Table 8. Recent revisions tend to lower the estimates for the gainfully occupied, and the correct total for 1938 would probably be between one and one and a half million less. On the other hand, the figure for estimated employment in 1919 should be raised slightly. However, the effect of these minor adjustments on the example in the text would be insignificant. The estimates of the gainfully occupied and employed used subsequently are all from *National Income and Its Composition*, without revisions.

TABLE 23

Illustrative Calculation of Difference between Potential Secular Levels
and Actual Levels of National Income, 1919-1938
(all dollar values in 1929 prices, billions)

	INDEXES OF POTENTIAL SECULAR MOVEMENT			POTENTIAL NATIONAL INCOME 1ST APPROX. (4)	DIFFERENCE BETWEEN ACTUAL & (4) (5)	POTENTIAL NATIONAL INCOME 2D APPROX. (6)	DIFFERENCE BETWEEN ACTUAL & (6) (7)
	Number of Gainfully Occupied (1)	Income per Employed (2)	National Income (3)				
1919	100.0	100.0	100	58.4	—0.2	58.4	—0.2
1920	101.9	101.7	104	60.7	—1.1	60.2	—0.6
1921	103.9	103.5	107.5	62.8	—6.5	62.5	—6.2
1922	105.8	105.2	111	64.8	—4.1	64.2	—3.5
1923	107.7	107.0	115	67.2	+3.1	66.6	+3.7
1924	109.6	108.7	119	69.5	+2.2	68.3	+3.4
1925	111.6	110.5	123	71.8	+2.2	70.7	+3.3
1926	113.5	112.2	127	74.2	+4.8	73.0	+6.0
1927	115.4	113.9	131	76.5	+3.4	74.8	+5.1
1928	117.3	115.7	136	79.4	+1.4	77.1	+3.7
1929	119.0	117.4	140	81.8	+5.1	79.4	+7.5
1930	120.3	119.2	143	83.5	—3.6	81.2	—1.3
1931	121.6	120.9	147	85.8	—17.1	82.9	—14.2
1932	122.9	122.7	151	88.2	—32.7	85.3	—29.8
1933	124.2	124.4	154.5	90.2	—33.9	87.0	—30.7
1934	125.5	126.2	158	92.3	—29.3	88.8	—25.8
1935	126.8	127.9	162	94.6	—27.0	90.5	—22.9
1936	128.1	129.6	166	96.9	—19.1	92.9	—15.1
1937	129.4	131.4	170	99.3	—15.3	94.6	—10.6
1938	130.7	133.1	174	101.6	—20.9	96.9	—16.2

COLUMN

1 The over-all percentage increase in the number of gainfully occupied between 1919-20 and 1928-29 and between 1928-29 and 1937-38 was calculated from estimates in *National Income and Its Composition,* Vol. One, Table 8. It checks fairly closely with the rate from 1920 to 1930 derived from *Normal Growth of the Labor Force in the United States: 1940 to 1950* (Bureau of the Census, Special Report, June 12, 1944), Table 5, p. 4; and from 1930 to 1940 derived from the same table on the basis of the increase in the "persons in labor force". The increase, prorated per year, was applied to 100.0 in 1919, to yield the entries for other years. Because it reflects some short term fluctuations associated with cycles, the actual annual series was not used.

2 Income per employed (in 1929 prices) was calculated for 1919, 1920, 1937, and 1938 from the annual estimates of national income in *National Product since 1869,* Table I 19, col. 3, and of aggregate employment in *National Income and Its Composition,* Vol. One, Table 8. The over-all percentage increase between the average for 1919-20 and that for 1937-38 was computed, prorated per year, and applied cumulatively to the 100.0 base for 1919.

3 Col. 1 multiplied by col. 2, divided by 100.

4 1919 (the average of 1919, 1920 weighted twice, and 1921, from *National Product since 1869*) extrapolated by col. 3.

5 Difference between actual levels in *ibid.* and col. 4.

6 Similar to col. 4, but on the assumption that the absorbed unemployed in 1937-38 (excluding frictional unemployment) estimated to be about 18 percent of the

secular rise in national income yielded column 3, which, applied to the national income level in 1919, estimated at the average actually attained during the 1919-21 cycle, yielded column 4— the potential secular level of national income in 1929 prices, on the assumption that the capacity level in 1919 is measured by the average for the cycle 1919-21, and that the two factors making for the secular rise are as estimated in columns 1 and 2.

The decade average for the 1920's shows no net deficit: on the contrary, in most years the actual level attained is above secular capacity, a result far from absurd since an economy can exceed its longer term capacity levels for a few years. The huge deficits appear with the 1929-32 depression, and persist, though they are much smaller from 1934 through 1938. The average deficit for the two decades is substantial—about $9.4 billion, or somewhat more than 13 percent of the average national income. It is the concentration of shortages in the 1930's that points at the crux of the business cycle problem in recent years—the persistent falling short of potential capacity levels during the last decade before this war.

Column 4 exaggerates the potential levels of national income in all years, particularly during recent years of large unemployment because it assigns income per employed to the gainfully occupied under the assumption of full employment (excluding a frictional minimum). This can be seen clearly when the shortages in 1937 and 1938 in column 5—about 22 percent of the national income actually attained—are compared with the relative unemployment in the two years. The latter, excluding frictional unemployment—estimated to be about 4 percent of the gainfully occupied—would amount to about 23 percent of total employment. In other words, the levels set in column 4 for 1937 and 1938 (and for other years) are those

Notes to Table 23 concluded
total gainfully occupied, can be assigned only 75 percent of the per capita income of those actually employed during these years. The reduced increase between 1919-20 and 1937-38 in income per employed was prorated and applied as in the calculation of col. 2. The resulting index multiplied by col. 1 and divided by 100 yielded a new column paralleling col. 3, which was then applied to 1919, col. 4.

that would be attained were we to assume full employment (excluding a frictional minimum); and income per absorbed unemployed equal to income per actually employed, at its secular level.

But in view of the selectivity possible when there is a large idle labor reserve, are we justified in assuming that income per absorbed unemployed would equal that actually received per employed? It is perhaps more reasonable to say that since most of the unemployed are the less qualified and skilled elements in the labor supply, they could be expected, if absorbed, to produce and receive a per capita income smaller than that of the actually employed. If we assume that the absorbed unemployed are unlikely to produce a per capita income larger than 75 percent of that per employed, the productivity index in later years and the implicit rise in productivity from 1919-20 (years of relatively full employment) to 1937-38, will be lowered. The effect of this assumption is to lower the level of the potential secular rise in national income (col. 6), reducing in turn the average deficit of actual income as compared with the potential (col. 7) to $7.2 billion, or somewhat above 10 percent of the average level; but the concentration of the deficits in the 1930's still remains.

Numerous objections—some apparent, some real—can be raised to the illustrative calculations in Table 23. It may be argued that capacity levels are set too low for 1919, thereby understating potential levels and deficits throughout the period. However valid the argument, the too low level in column 4 for 1919 is not due to cyclical causes: the 1921 depression, as measured by indexes of physical volume, is not one of the more violent, and low capacity during the 1919-21 cycle would be due to after-effects of the war, not to cyclical factors.

Among the more real objections is that the rates of increase in the gainfully occupied and in income per employed are taken from an historical period in which business cycles are conspicuous. Were we to wish away cycles completely, productivity might rise because of an uninterrupted net cumulation of capital and of consumer demand assuring steadily expanding markets, much more than it does in column 2. The difficulty with this argument is that it goes into realms of speculation, where no conclusion can be proved or disproved. For example, one could argue that were cycles wished completely away, rates of labor market participation might drop and the gainfully occupied and hours of employment be appreciably fewer than they actually were. This would mean a lowering of the index in column 1 that might offset or more than offset the argued greater rise of the index in column 2.

If we accept the framework of the analysis illustrated in Table 23—and the loss entailed by cyclical depressions can be calculated only if one accepts some realistic measures of capacity factors—two conclusions of interest emerge. First, the loss, in the sense of an average deficit in actual national product as compared with that possible by steady growth from the 1919 levels, is much less, in percentage terms, than one would be likely to guess, particularly because the depressed 1930's are remembered more vividly than the expansive 1920's. Second, the deficits are concentrated in the 1930's and this raises the serious problem, already noted in Part II in the discussion of longer term trends, as to the secular significance of this decade, i.e., does it represent retardation of growth, portending lower secular levels for the future?

Whatever the judgment, Tables 22 and 23 clearly indicate that marked short term fluctuations in total production and employment are concomitants of business cycles; that though the gaps they cause between actual and potential national income levels may not average out to large percentages, the deficits may be substantial, and in the 1930's, were huge. Again, there is a sizable loss to social welfare from the mere fluctuations in volumes and rates of change, regardless of their effect on long term levels. In explaining and dealing with these cyclical fluctuations, differences in the consistency and amplitude with which business cycles are reflected in various sectors of the economy are important.

2 National Aggregates, in Current and Constant Prices

Table 24 summarizes changes during business cycles in three nationwide aggregates in current prices; and in the most com-

TABLE 24

National Income and Aggregate Payments, Differences in Rate of
Movement between Expansion and Contraction
Reference Cycles, 1919-1938
(all measures of change are on a per year basis and in percentages of
the average value of the series for each full reference cycle)

| | | | AGGREGATE PAYMENTS | | |
REFERENCE CYCLES	NATIONAL INCOME Current Prices (1)	INCL. ENTREP. SAVINGS Current Prices (2)	EXCL. ENTREP. SAVINGS Current Prices (3)	NATIONAL INCOME 1929 Prices (4)
1 1919-21	—36.5	—27.3	—33.2	—8.2
2 1921-24	—8.5	—7.4	—6.6	—8.7
3 1924-27	—7.9	—4.7	—2.5	—3.5
4 1927-32	—24.9	—20.3	—18.1	—18.2
5 1932-38	—19.0	—16.4	—14.6	—12.9
6 Av. for 5 cycles	—19.4	—15.2	—15.0	—10.3

COLUMN
1-3 *National Income and Its Composition,* Vol. One, Table 3.
4 Based on estimates in *National Product since 1869,* Table I 19, col. 3.

prehensive of the three, national income, in 1929 prices. The
measures used—differences between the change per year during expansion and during contraction, the changes expressed in
percentages of the average value for each reference cycle—are
most free from the effect of longer term movements and therefore most suitable for studying the consistency with which a
series reflects business cycles and the amplitude of its fluctuation during reference cycle periods.[26]

The three countrywide totals in current prices differ in that
national income (col. 1) includes undistributed net profits of

[26]The differences referred to and used in all the subsequent tables are calculated
as follows. The values for each series are converted to percentages of the average
value for each reference cycle. The total change in these percentages from the
reference year of the initial cyclical trough to the reference year of the cyclical
peak, divided by the number of years elapsed, is the change per year during
the reference cycle expansion. The total change from the reference year of the
cyclical peak to the reference year of the terminal cyclical trough, divided by
the number of years elapsed, is the change per year during the reference
cycle contraction. The difference in the rate of movement is then calculated by
subtracting the change per year during the reference cycle expansion from the
change per year during the reference cycle contraction.

These calculations are made for each reference cycle separately. The averages
are arithmetic means of the measures for the several reference cycles occurring in
the period.

corporations and net savings of governments; aggregate payments in column 2 exclude these items but, like column 1,
include entrepreneurial net savings; column 3, by means of
a rough segregation of entrepreneurial withdrawals from net
income, excludes entrepreneurial net savings. Differences among
the three totals in their changes during business cycles must
be due to the cyclical behavior of items excluded from one
total and included in another.

Consequently, the very substantial narrowing, as we pass
from national income to aggregate payments including entrepreneurial savings, in the amplitude of the 'differential' change
during business cycles—from an average of —19.4 to —15.2—
is due to the extreme sensitivity of net savings of corporations
(and to some extent of government savings) to business cycles.
Since this item constitutes merely a small percentage of national
income, its fluctuations during business cycles must be violent
indeed for its exclusion to narrow so appreciably the amplitude
of the differential movement. And, in fact, as the economy
expands and contracts, net savings of corporations move from
large positive to large negative totals. The exclusion of them
(and of government savings) narrows the amplitude of movement in all five reference cycles.

One would expect that the exclusion of entrepreneurial net
savings would also narrow the amplitude of the differential
movement during business cycles: these savings or undistributed
net profits should vary more intensely than most distributed
income flows. And, indeed, the averages excluding entrepreneurial net savings are slightly smaller in four of the five
reference cycles. The narrowing in amplitude is not greater
partly because of the large weight in entrepreneurial net savings
of those by farmers: farm incomes in general do not move in
consistent conformity with business cycles.

That a substantial part of the changes in national income
during business cycles is due to fluctuations in prices is evident
when estimates in current and in 1929 prices are compared
(col. 1 and 4). Adjustment for price changes cuts the average
for the five reference cycles almost in half and causes a reduction in four of the five cycles. The reduction is particularly

large in the 1919-21 swing, which was characterized by violent
changes in price levels.

Robert F. Martin's estimates, used in Part II, are analyzed
here to measure the changes during business cycles for a longer
period, covering ten rather than five reference cycles (Table
25). His totals are comparable to our aggregate payments
excluding entrepreneurial net savings; and thus represent the
least cyclically-sensitive of the three countrywide totals in
Table 24.

TABLE 25

Aggregate Payments excluding Entrepreneurial Savings
Differences in Rate of Movement between Expansion and Contraction
Reference Cycles, 1900-1938

(all measures of change are on a per year basis and in percentages of
the average value of the series for each full reference cycle)

REFERENCE CYCLES		CURRENT PRICES (1)	1929 PRICES (2)
1	1900-04	—3.5	+0.5
2	1904-08	—10.5	—3.1
3	1908-11	—9.0	—6.4
4	1911-14	—6.3	—6.4
5	1914-19	—1.0	—7.6
6	1919-21	—26.9	+3.4
7	1921-24	—5.1	—7.5
8	1924-27	—3.9	—0.2
9	1927-32	—19.7	—13.6
10	1932-38	—18.8	—13.2
	Averages		
11	Lines 1-10	—10.5	—5.4
12	1- 5	—6.1	—4.6
13	6-10	—14.9	—6.2
14	1- 4	—7.3	—3.9
15	4- 7	—9.8	—4.5
16	7-10	—11.9	—8.6

Based on estimates in R. F. Martin, *National Income in the United States, 1799-
1938,* Table 1, and revisions in the *Economic Almanac for 1944-45* (National
Industrial Conference Board, 1944), p. 80. Mr. Martin's series in 1926 prices was
recomputed to a 1929 base.

When measured in current prices, these countrywide aggregates of income payments reflect all ten reference cycles. But
when a crude adjustment for price changes is made, the rate
of change from expansion to contraction apparently does not
decline in two reference cycles, possibly because of the crudity
of either the current price estimates or of the price adjust-

ment. On the other hand, it may well be that in a mild business cycle such as 1900-04 the rate of change in annual totals of income payments, expressed in units of constant purchasing power, does not decline from expansion to contraction.[27]

The adjustment for price changes results not only in failure to reflect every business cycle in the period but also in a much narrower amplitude of the differential change. The average for the ten cycles declines almost one-half from column 1 to column 2; and this narrowing of amplitude is observed in seven of the ten reference cycles.

Though the period is only 38 years the amplitude of the changes during reference cycles may be studied for some trend. Do the fluctuations, as measured by the degree to which the rate of change declines from reference expansion to contraction, become more or less prominent over the period?

For the aggregates in current prices, the answer is clear: the amplitude of the differential change does widen perceptibly from the earlier part of the period to the later, whether we group the ten cycles in two sets of five or in three sets of four with one overlapping. But this uptrend in amplitude seems to be due in large part to price fluctuations. For the totals in constant prices, the amplitudes widen much less. The average for the first five cycles is —4.6; for the second five, —6.2. In the three groups of four cycles each, a moderate widening of amplitude from the first to the second is followed by a very substantial widening from the second to the third. However, because the estimates for recent years are more accurate, they may be expected to reflect cyclical changes more sensitively. Hence this widening in amplitude may, at least in part, be due to the statistical improvement of the estimates; and cannot be taken as evidence of an appreciable secular rise in the amplitude of changes during business cycles in totals in constant prices. The sole unambiguous evidence lies in the length of the 1929-32 contraction, the one reference contraction in the

[27] A comparison with Table 24 shows no exception for the 1919-21 cycle for *national income* in constant prices. This suggests that were the estimates in Table 25, col. 2 for national income instead of for aggregate payments, they would probably have conformed in all reference cycles.

period that in the annual chronology lasts more than a year.

3 Differences among Industries

From what we know about the cyclical behavior of various
industries, we would expect marked differences among them
in the degree to which the rate of change in their activity
fluctuates with cycles in the economy at large. And we do find
such marked differences in the estimates of the net product
of each industry (i.e., its gross product minus the contribution to it of other industries consumed in the production
process) in current prices, for the five reference cycles of
1919-38 (Table 26). Even for the ten broad industrial divisions, differences in the amplitude of fluctuations during business cycles are large. As judged by the averages for the
period, the industrial divisions whose fluctuations during business cycles are distinctly narrower than in the all-industry
average are the various service groups (finance—covering
banking, insurance, and real estate—service, and government)
and trade. Of the commodity producing divisions agriculture
alone shows a smaller average change than all industries
combined. The changes in mining, manufacturing, and construction, on the contrary, have an amplitude well above the
all-industry average.

These differences among the major industrial divisions tend
to persist from cycle to cycle. The entry for government is
lower than that for the all-industry average in four of the five
cycles; for service—in four of the five, and equal to the all-industry average in the fifth; for finance—in all five; for trade and
agriculture—in three of the five. The industrial divisions characterized by amplitudes wider than that for the all-industry average, mining, manufacturing, and construction, show it in all
five reference cycles.

Changes during business cycles in net income originating
in many other, more narrowly defined, industrial branches can
be estimated from the data in *National Income and Its Composition*. Those selected here illustrate the contrasts among
branches within the major industrial divisions—primarily between industries supplying ultimate consumers and industrial

TABLE 26

Net Income Originating (Current Prices) by Industries
Differences in Rate of Movement between Expansion and Contraction
Reference Cycles, 1919-1938

(all measures of change are on a per year basis and in percentages of
the average value of the series for each full reference cycle)

INDUSTRIAL DIVISIONS	REFERENCE CYCLES					AV. FOR 5 CYCLES
	1919-21 (1)	1921-24 (2)	1924-27 (3)	1927-32 (4)	1932-38 (5)	(6)
1 Agriculture	—20.3	—3.3	—3.8	—29.2	—30.0	—17.3
2 Mining	—94.4	—35.8	—34.3	—36.8	—55.4	—51.3
3 Manufacturing	—54.6	—35.1	—8.7	—42.1	—56.5	—39.4
4 Construction	—56.4	—15.1	—11.6	—32.2	—25.0	—28.1
5 Transp. & other public utilities	—39.6	—7.8	—6.6	—21.4	—18.2	—18.7
6 Trade	—11.9	—21.3	—6.3	—24.1	—13.5	—15.4
7 Finance	—4.9	+2.9	+4.0	—24.2	—5.8	—5.6
8 Service	—14.0	—5.4	—5.5	—21.4	—10.7	—11.4
9 Government	—67.7	+9.8	—0.6	—13.4	—9.7	—16.3
10 Miscellaneous	—21.8	—13.2	—7.2	—38.7	—21.0	—20.4
11 Total	—34.6	—14.2	—5.6	—27.4	—23.8	—21.1
Branches						
2a Anthracite mining	—14.8	+7.0	—20.8	—9.9	—18.9	—11.5
2b Metal mining	—99.7	—30.5	—19.5	—99.9	—137.0	—77.3
3a Food & tobacco mfg.	—16.1	—16.0	+0.8	—24.7	—14.3	—14.1
3b Metal mfg.	—79.5	—43.4	—14.6	—60.0	—96.8	—58.9
5a Steam rr., Pullman & express	—44.4	—11.8	—9.0	—24.6	—27.6	—23.5
5b Street railways	—19.9	—6.5	—0.7	—12.9	—2.5	—8.5
5c Telephone	—9.3	—0.7	—2.8	—17.4	—3.8	—6.8

Based on data underlying Table 59, *National Income and Its Composition*, Vol. One.

users. Anthracite mining has a relatively narrow amplitude; metal mining, a wide amplitude. The difference is almost as great between changes during business cycles in net income originating in the food and tobacco and in the metal manufacturing industries. In the public utilities group, net income originating in steam railroads changes much more during business cycles than that originating in street railways or telephones. All these inter-industry differences in the degree to which their activity reflects business cycles are fairly persistent, cycle by cycle.

To extend the record we use Robert F. Martin's estimates since 1900. As his series is of aggregate payments excluding entrepreneurial savings, not of national income, the estimates in Table 27 are of changes in total payments, not in net in-

TABLE 27

Total Payments excluding Entrepreneurial Savings
(Current Prices) by Industries, Differences in Rate of Movement
between Expansion and Contraction, Reference Cycles, 1900-1938
(all measures of change are on a per year basis and in percentages of
the average value of the series for each full reference cycle)

| | MARTIN'S SERIES, AV. FOR | | NBER SERIES, AV. FOR | |
INDUSTRIAL DIVISIONS	5 Reference Cycles 1900-19 (1)	4 Reference Cycles 1919-32 (2)	4 Reference Cycles 1919-32 (3)	5 Reference Cycles 1919-38 (4)
1 Agriculture	—3.0	—8.0	—17.1	—15.1
2 Mining	—26.4	—33.3	—29.7	—32.0
3 Manufacturing	—15.4	—25.0	—24.9	—28.7
4 Construction	—6.9	—28.5	—28.4	—26.9
5 Transp. & other public utilities	—2.2	—13.7	—14.9	—14.2
6 Trade	—1.8	—13.1	—13.7	—12.6
7 Finance	+2.2	—8.5	—5.6	—4.5
8 Service	+0.5	—9.6	—8.5	—8.8
9 Government	—5.6	+3.1	+0.3	+0.6
10 Miscellaneous	—8.0	—9.0	—10.5	—10.7
11 Total	—6.1	—13.9	—15.1	—15.0

COLUMN
1 & 2 Based on estimates in *National Income in the United States, 1799-1938*,
Tables 1, 19, 21, 23, 25, 27, 29, 31, 33, 35, 37, 39, 40, 43, 44, and 46.
3 & 4 Based on data underlying Table 61, *National Income and Its Composition*,
Vol. One.

come, originating in the major industrial divisions (the latter
alone are available).

The averages indicate that the changes in the rate of movement from expansion to contraction were, with two exceptions
(finance and service), of the same sign, if not of the same
magnitude, during the five cycles from 1900 through 1919.
Too, the inter-industry differences in the amplitude of the
changes observed in Table 26 persist. In government, service,
finance, trade, agriculture, and also—more conspicuously here
than in Table 26—the public utilities group, the rate of change
from expansion to contraction is much smaller, on the average, than in the all-industry average (col. 1). In mining,
manufacturing, and construction, it is distinctly larger.

Moreover, the amplitude widens from the five reference
cycles of 1900-19 (col. 1) to the four of 1919-32 (col. 2);
and by implication to the five of 1919-38. For every industrial
division except government, the average differential movement

during business cycles for the first twenty years is appreciably less than for the second. Thus, the widening in the amplitude of aggregate payments in current prices in Table 25 is seen here to be true of payments originating in each of the ten major industrial divisions. There is some doubt about the existence of such a trend in the totals in constant prices. But violent fluctuations even in monetary totals are significant, so far as they create stresses and strains in the credit and money mechanism, and thus tend to affect eventually the flows measured in real terms.

Since there are appreciable differences in the extent to which the prices of products or resources in various industries fluctuate during business cycles, estimates of net product in constant prices would not show the same inter-industry differences as do those in current prices in Tables 26 and 27. In the absence of net income estimates by industries in constant prices, we use total employment. True, employment tends to vary less during business cycles than net income in constant prices: the average decline in the rate of change from expansion to contraction 1919-38 was 10.3 for national income in constant prices and 7.6 for aggregate employment. Yet, inter-industry differences in changes in net product in constant prices are likely to be associated with inter-industry differences in changes in employment (Table 28).

Comparison of Tables 28 and 26 reveals interesting similarities and differences. As in the case of net income in current prices, the fluctuations in employment during business cycles have a narrower amplitude than the average for all industries in all services (service, government, finance), trade, and agriculture; and a wider amplitude than the average in mining, manufacturing, and construction. Again, as in Table 26, these differences in amplitude are fairly consistent from cycle to cycle. Here also, as in Table 26, the branches of mining, manufacturing, and public utilities, singled out to illustrate differences between consumer and producer goods categories, show the expected contrasts in amplitude of fluctuations during business cycles, both in the averages and consistently cycle by cycle.

But it is the differences between Tables 26 and 28 that

TABLE 28

Total Employment by Industries, Differences in Rate of Movement
between Expansion and Contraction, Reference Cycles, 1919-1938
(all measures of change are on a per year basis and in percentages of
the average value of the series for each full reference cycle)

INDUSTRIAL DIVISIONS	REFERENCE CYCLES					AV. FOR 5 CYCLES
	1919-21 (1)	1921-24 (2)	1924-27 (3)	1927-32 (4)	1932-38 (5)	(6)
1 Agriculture	—1.5	+0.5	—1.3	—0.2	—0.2	—0.5
2 Mining	—38.4	—21.6	—15.2	—10.5	—20.7	—21.3
3 Manufacturing	—22.1	—17.6	—4.0	—17.5	—27.7	—17.8
4 Construction	—21.4	—14.0	—13.6	—23.2	—16.9	—17.8
5 Transp. & other public utilities	—22.2	—8.3	—2.7	—11.5	—13.2	—11.6
6 Trade	—16.0	—2.4	+0.7	—10.3	—6.2	—6.8
7 Finance	—8.7	+4.6	+3.7	—13.3	—2.4	—3.2
8 Service	—2.2	—1.9	—0.5	—8.5	—6.9	—4.0
9 Government	+21.6	+5.3	+0.5	—1.5	—1.5	+4.9
10 Miscellaneous	—4.0	—5.1	—1.8	—8.2	—5.5	—4.9
11 Total	—10.4	—6.0	—2.3	—9.5	—9.9	—7.6
Branches						
2a Anthracite mining	+18.9	+9.1	+4.2	—6.6	—9.7	+3.2
2b Metal mining	—48.3	—25.6	—9.1	—23.7	—51.5	—31.6
3a Food & tobacco mfg.	—9.4	—7.6	+3.1	—11.0	—11.4	—7.3
3b Metal mfg.	—42.0	—26.7	—8.3	—27.6	—47.9	—30.5
5a Steam rr., Pullman & express	—25.1	—10.6	—3.3	—11.3	—18.2	—13.7
5b Street railways	—10.9	—6.0	—1.3	—7.3	—1.5	—5.4
5c Telephone	—12.8	—5.2	—0.6	—16.3	—1.8	—7.3

Based on data underlying Table 69, *National Income and Its Composition*, Vol. One.

suggest the effect of price fluctuations on changes in net income in current prices. For employment, the average amplitude of changes in agriculture falls much further short of
that for the all-industry average than for net income in current prices in Table 26. Obviously, prices of agricultural products tend to fluctuate with the business cycles, affecting net
income originating in agriculture in current prices; and probably the average changes in the net product of agriculture in
constant prices during business cycles would have much narrower amplitudes than those in national income in constant
prices. A difference of opposite character appears for the
transportation and public utilities category: the amplitude of
the fluctuations in its employment during business cycles is
appreciably wider than in all-industry employment, in both
the average and in all five reference cycles (except 1924-27

where the difference is still of the same sign, but small). Net income in current prices originating in this category was shown in Table 26 to fluctuate during business cycles with an amplitude somewhat narrower than that in national income, both in the average for the period and in three of the five reference cycles. Presumably the temporal stability of prices for services of transportation and public utilities and hence their lesser responsiveness to business cycles affects fluctuations in net income in current prices; so that changes in net income in constant prices in that industry may well be of appreciably wider amplitude than those in national income in constant prices.

The declines in the rate of change from reference expansion to contraction, in both net income and employment, suggest two tentative conclusions. First, while the amplitude of change during business cycles is very much wider in net income (current prices) than in employment, the *relative* dispersion among the various industries appears to be wider for employment than for net income. For example, in employment (Table 28, col. 6) the average decline in the rate of change from expansion to contraction is 7.6 for all industries (as a percentage of the average value for each reference cycle); but the range among industrial divisions is from +4.9 to —21.3. In net income (Table 26, col. 6) the all-industry average is —21.1; but the range, from —5.6 to —51.3, is relatively narrower than in employment.

Second, distinct differences appear among the successive reference cycles in the relative dispersion among industries of the measures of 'differential' change, in both net income and employment. For example, for the 1919-21 cycle, the cyclical change in net income for the all-industry average is —34.6, with a range among industrial divisions from —4.9 to —94.4; for the 1927-32 cycle, when the all-industry average is —27.4, the range is only from —13.4 to —42.1. For employment there is a similar contrast in the inter-industry dispersion of measures of change: for the 1919-21 cycle the all-industry entry is —10.4, the range, from +21.6 to —38.4; for the 1927-32 cycle it is —9.5, with a range from —0.2 to —23.2.

These two conclusions are confirmed by simple measures of inter-industry dispersion in changes during business cycles (Table 29). One set was calculated by using the ten major industrial divisions shown in the earlier tables; the other set, covering thirty industrial divisions, by using also the minor industrial groups, when available (only such major groups were included as were not available by subgroups). For each cycle and for the average of the five cycles the unweighted all-industry arithmetic mean was computed (lines 1, 4, 7, and 10); the average deviation from the arithmetic mean (lines 2, 5, 8, and 11); and as a measure of relative dispersion, the ratio of the average deviation to the unweighted mean (lines 3, 6, 9, and 12).

In every comparison based on the major industrial divisions, the relative dispersion among industries in the amplitude of change during business cycles is greater for employment than for net income in current prices; in the comparison based on the major and minor industrial divisions, it is greater for the all-industry average and for three of the five reference cycles. This suggests that the cyclical price changes, which tend to be common to all industries, contribute to greater convergence in changes during business cycles when measured in current prices. In employment, this common influence of price change is missing. One might expect that, were estimates of net income in constant prices available, the changes in them during business cycles would also show greater relative dispersion among industries than the changes in income in current prices.

The second conclusion is likewise confirmed and extended: differences among the several cycles in the inter-industry dispersion of declines in the rate of movement from expansion to contraction are evident. For both net income in current prices and employment, this inter-industry dispersion is greater in the first three reference cycles than in the last two; and in both the broader and the more detailed industrial classifications. What distinguishes the last two reference cycles from the first three is their much longer duration: the 1927-32 cycle lasted five years, the 1932-38 cycle, six, whereas the first

TABLE 29

Net Income Originating (Current Prices) and Total Employment
Inter-industry Dispersion in Magnitude of Changes during
Reference Cycles, 1919-1938
(based on changes in rate of movement from expansion to contraction)

| | REFERENCE CYCLES | | | | | AV. FOR 5 CYCLES |
	1919-21 (1)	1921-24 (2)	1924-27 (3)	1927-32 (4)	1932-38 (5)	(6)
A TEN MAJOR INDUSTRIAL DIVISIONS						
Net Income Originating						
1 Unweighted mean	38.6	12.4	8.1	28.4	24.6	22.4
2 Av. deviation from line 1	24.0	11.7	6.1	7.4	13.7	10.3
3 Relative dispersion (line 2 ÷ line 1)	0.62	0.94	0.76	0.26	0.56	0.46
Total Employment						
4 Unweighted mean	11.5	6.0	3.4	10.5	10.1	7.3
5 Av. deviation from line 4	12.5	7.4	4.5	4.7	7.6	7.8
6 Relative dispersion (line 5 ÷ line 4)	1.09	1.23	1.32	0.45	0.75	1.07
B THIRTY MAJOR AND MINOR INDUSTRIAL DIVISIONS						
Net Income Originating						
7 Unweighted mean	47.6	15.3	10.2	30.1	31.7	27.0
8 Av. deviation from line 7	34.4	15.6	11.3	13.0	21.1	17.2
9 Relative dispersion (line 8 ÷ line 7)	0.72	1.02	1.11	0.43	0.67	0.64
Total Employment						
10 Unweighted mean	14.7	8.6	3.4	11.8	14.2	10.5
11 Av. deviation from line 10	14.9	8.8	5.3	5.6	9.6	7.6
12 Relative dispersion (line 11 ÷ line 10)	1.01	1.03	1.58	0.47	0.67	0.73

LINE

1 & 7 Based on data underlying Table 59, *National Income and Its Composition,*
Vol. One. The minus signs for these entries have been omitted.

4 & 10 Based on data underlying Table 69, *ibid;* minus signs omitted.

three reference cycles lasted two, three, and three years, respectively. In other words, the longer the cycle, the more time there is for the cyclical effects to materialize not only in the industries highly sensitive but also in those relatively insensitive to fluctuations in general business. Because of 'ceilings' and 'floors' limiting the amplitude of cyclical expansions and contractions in various industries, a long reference cycle means less inter-industry dispersion than a short.

In the brief record in Table 29, the duration of the cycle

is more important than the intensity of the fluctuation in determining inter-industry dispersion. One would expect that the
more violent the cycle, the more consistently would all industries be affected, and the less the inter-industry dispersion
in the amplitude of the 'differential' change. Yet the 1919-21
reference cycle, though characterized by a greater decline in
the rate of movement from expansion to contraction than the
1927-32 and 1932-38 cycles, shows relative inter-industry dispersion greater rather than less than for the last two.

4   *Differences among Types of Payment*
We should not expect income flows of different types—wages,
salaries, dividends, interest, etc.—to respond to business
cycles with the same consistency and amplitude. Some, such as
interest and salaries, are, by reason of social or institutional
inertia, sticky and unresponsive to short term changes. Others,
such as entrepreneurial income, are heavily weighted by agriculture, whose short term fluctuations do not conform closely
to reference cycles. Still others, such as dividends, which are
in part akin to entrepreneurial profits and concentrated in
mining and manufacturing—both industries quite responsive
to business cycles—can be expected to show consistent and
large variations in the rate of movement within reference
cycles.

The estimates in Table 30 for the five reference cycles from
1919 through 1938 do show differences in average amplitude
that fulfil these expectations. In dividends the average change
in rate of movement from expansion to contraction is a large
decline, much greater than in aggregate payments. The only
other type of payment showing an amplitude wider than in
the aggregate payments average is employee compensation,
presumably because of the sensitivity of wages in such cyclically responsive industries as mining, manufacturing, construction,
and some public utilities. In dividends, the amplitude of the
changes is wider than in aggregate payments in three of the
five reference cycles, in employee compensation in only two.

Of the three other types of payment, two—interest and
rent—show changes during business cycles of distinctly, and

TABLE 30

Various Types of Income Payment (Current Prices)
Differences in Rate of Movement between Expansion
and Contraction, Reference Cycles, 1919-1938
(all measures of change are on a per year basis and in percentages of
the average value of the series for each full reference cycle)

TYPES OF INCOME PAYMENT	REFERENCE CYCLES					AV. FOR 5 CYCLES
	1919-21 (1)	1921-24 (2)	1924-27 (3)	1927-32 (4)	1932-38 (5)	(6)
1 Employee compensation	—37.7	—9.8	—4.2	—19.0	—16.4	—17.4
2 Entrep. net income						
a Incl. savings	—13.2	—4.1	—12.1	—25.9	—14.8	—14.0
b Excl. savings	—40.0	+0.6	—0.7	—13.0	—4.7	—11.6
3 Service income						
a Incl. entrep. savings	—31.1	—8.5	—6.0	—20.4	—16.2	—16.4
b Excl. entrep. savings	—38.2	—7.6	—3.4	—17.7	—14.1	—16.2
4 Dividends	—19.0	—13.5	—2.9	—32.5	—49.7	—23.5
5 Interest	—5.7	0.0	+1.6	—7.7	+1.5	—2.1
6 Rent	—3.2	+2.4	+3.4	—20.8	—4.6	—4.6
7 Property income incl. rent	—8.5	—2.7	+0.9	—19.7	—17.5	—9.5
8 Aggregate payments						
a Incl. entrep. savings	—27.3	—7.4	—4.7	—20.3	—16.4	—15.2
b Excl. entrep. savings	—33.2	—6.6	—2.5	—18.1	—14.6	—15.0

LINE

1-7 Based on estimates in *National Income and Its Composition*, Vol. One,
    Tables 1 and 57.
8a & b *Ibid.*, Table 3.

on the whole consistently, narrower applitude than those
characterizing aggregate payments. The average for interest
is less than one-seventh of that for aggregate payments; for
rent, somewhat less than one-third. Interest shows this narrower amplitude of change in all five reference cycles; rent,
in four.

The average amplitude of changes in entrepreneurial income is narrower than in aggregate payments, and this narrower amplitude is observed in four of the five cycles if
savings are excluded; in only three if savings are included. Possibly agriculture causes large variations in this type of payment when it expands and contracts with business at large;
and small variations when it runs counter to the short term
trend of the urban economy, as happens at least part of the time.

The *average* differences among types of payment in the
amplitude of change during the five reference cycles 1919-38

are true also of their cyclical behavior during the first two
decades of the century (Table 31). Here again, the rate of
movement in dividends fluctuated more violently than in
aggregate payments or in any other type of payment. In the
least sensitive, interest and rent, the rate of movement in this
earlier period from expansion to contraction does not decline
on the average. The average for employee compensation exceeds that for aggregate payments; for entrepreneurial income (excluding net savings) it is less.

TABLE 31

Various Types of Income Payment (Current Prices)

Differences in Rate of Movement between Expansion
and Contraction, Reference Cycles, 1900-1938

(all measures of change are on a per year basis and in percentages of
the average value of the series for each full reference cycle)

	MARTIN'S SERIES, AV. FOR		NBER SERIES, AV. FOR	
	5 Reference Cycles	4 Reference Cycles	4 Reference Cycles	5 Reference Cycles
TYPES OF INCOME PAYMENT	1900-19	1919-32	1919-32	1919-38
	(1)	(2)	(3)	(4)
1 Employee compensation	—7.4	—16.8	—17.7	—17.4
2 Entrep. withdrawals	—3.8	—6.5	—13.3	—11.6
3 Service income	—6.5	—14.9	—16.7	—16.2
4 Dividends	—16.9	—9.6	—17.0	—23.5
5 Interest	+4.3	—5.5	—2.9	—2.1
6 Rent	+1.4	—9.7	—4.6	—4.6
7 Property income incl. rent	—4.3	—8.1	—7.5	—9.5
8 Aggregate payments excl. entrep. savings	—6.1	—13.9	—15.1	—15.0

COLUMN
1 & 2 Based on estimates in *National Income in the United States, 1799-1938*,
  Tables 4, 41, 42, 43, 44, 46.
3 & 4 Based on estimates in *National Income and Its Composition*, Vol. One,
  Table 57.

Types of payment differ also in the consistency with which
they fluctuate more or less than aggregate payments. For
example, dividends show a wider amplitude of change than
aggregate payments in four of the five reference cycles 1900-
19; and the amplitude of change in interest and in rent is
narrower than that for aggregate payments in all five cycles.
In contrast, the wider amplitude of change in employee com-

pensation, and the narrower in entrepreneurial income is observed in only three of the five reference cycles.

Finally, the most important difference among types of income in the degree of their participation in business cycles—that between undistributed net profits of corporations and all payment flows—is not measured in Tables 30 and 31. Because these undistributed net profits alternate from positive to negative figures, the technique of measuring changes during business cycles in *percentages* of cycle averages is not applicable to them. But as revealed by Table 24 above the wide amplitude of their fluctuations is manifest in the effect their inclusion with all payment flows to form national income has on the magnitude of changes in the latter.

5 Differences among Shares of Upper and Lower Income Groups

Differences in the degree to which types of payment vary during business cycles should provide some basis for conjecturing changes in the distribution of income among recipients grouped by size of income. As some types of payment flow chiefly to the upper and others chiefly to the lower income groups and the differences in the type-composition of income at the lower and at the upper levels are substantial, the wider amplitude of changes in dividends, narrower in interest, and so on, should give us some clue to the changes in the size distribution during business cycles.

But the inferences cannot be definitive, for the effects of the inter-type differences in amplitude are not all or even preponderantly in the same direction. The wider amplitude of changes in dividends would suggest that the share of total income payments going to the upper income groups should increase during expansions and decline during contractions. But the narrower amplitude of changes in interest and the wider amplitude of changes in employee compensation suggest that the differential movement in the share of the upper income groups should be an increase from expansion to contraction, not a decline.

The only data with which we can study these fluctuations

in the size distribution of total income payments during business cycles are those mentioned in Part I—federal income tax returns. As noted, comparison of the income tax population and its income with total population and total income payments yields approximations to the shares of income of the top 5 percent of population alone. But even a series that covers only the extreme upper right tail of the distribution may be of interest.

In order to simplify presentation and discussion, Tables 32 and 33 deal with the one variant of income shares of the upper income groups in the population for which analysis by type of payment is possible. This variant is not adjusted for differences between marital status groups in number of persons per return; nor to exclude federal income taxes. But these adjustments would not affect greatly the short term movements of the shares. A more important factor is that income receipts analyzed here exclude capital gains, gifts, and other transfers. In other words, they are shares in total income payments—not the amounts individuals retain after the kind of re-distribution that results from purchase and sale of assets, gifts, contributions, etc. The exclusion of capital gains in particular removes an important cyclical element in the distribution of income by size, when income is defined to include net results of transfers.[28]

The first impression produced by Table 32 is that annual shares in total income payments received by the upper 1 percent of population; by the next group of 2d through 5th percent from top; and by the whole mass of the lower 95 percent, fluctuate from year to year only moderately (col. 1, 5, and 9). There is no year in which the share in column 1 undergoes an absolute change of more than 1.5 percent; in

[28]Yet even the inclusion of capital gains would not invalidate the conclusions suggested below. It would serve largely to accentuate the short term fluctuations, shown by the variant analyzed in Tables 32 and 33, resulting particularly in a greater rise of the share of the upper 1 percent to 1928; and a more conspicuous decline of that share to the middle 1930's. This statement is based partly upon our own analysis, and partly on the estimates of Adolph J. Goldenthal (see *Concentration and Composition of Individual Incomes, 1918-1937*, TNEC Monograph No. 4, Washington, D. C., 1940).

TABLE 32

Annual Changes in Percentage Shares of Total Income Payments
(Current Prices) Received by Upper and Lower Income Groups, 1919-1938
(basic variant, unadjusted for marital status and including federal income taxes)

| | UPPER 1 PERCENT | | | | 2D THROUGH 5TH PERCENT FROM TOP | | | | LOWER 95 PERCENT | | | |
| | | | CHANGE ASSOCIATED WITH SHIFTS | | | | CHANGE ASSOCIATED WITH SHIFTS | | | | CHANGE ASSOCIATED WITH SHIFTS | |
	% SHARE IN TOTAL INCOME PAYMENTS (1)	CHANGE IN (1) (2)	Among Types of Payment (3)	Within Types of Payment (4)	% SHARE IN TOTAL INCOME PAYMENTS (5)	CHANGE IN (5) (6)	Among Types of Payment (7)	Within Types of Payment (8)	% SHARE IN TOTAL INCOME PAYMENTS (9)	CHANGE IN (9) (10)	Among Types of Payment (11)	Within Types of Payment (12)
1919	12.8				10.1				77.1			
1920	12.3	−0.50	−0.27	−0.23	9.7	−0.34	−0.16	−0.18	77.9	+0.84	+0.43	+0.41
1921	13.5	+1.16	+0.57	+0.58	12.0	+2.24	+1.65	+0.60	74.5	−3.40	−2.22	−1.18
1922	13.4	−0.12	−0.07	−0.05	11.4	−0.56	−0.45	−0.11	75.2	+0.68	+0.52	+0.16
1923	12.3	−1.10	−0.89	−0.21	10.6	−0.80	−0.60	−0.20	77.1	+1.90	+1.49	+0.41
1924	12.9	+0.63	+0.47	+0.17	11.4	+0.77	+0.53	+0.23	75.7	−1.40	−1.00	−0.40
1925	13.7	+0.82	+0.42	+0.40	11.5	+0.08	+0.06	+0.02	74.8	−0.90	−0.48	−0.42
1926	13.9	+0.20	+0.19	+0.01	11.3	−0.15	−0.06	−0.09	74.8	−0.05	−0.13	+0.08
1927	14.4	+0.46	+0.23	+0.22	11.6	+0.26	+0.21	+0.05	74.0	−0.72	−0.44	−0.27
1928	14.9	+0.56	+0.28	+0.27	11.8	+0.26	+0.20	+0.06	73.2	−0.81	−0.48	−0.33
1929	14.5	−0.45	−0.49	+0.05	11.6	−0.24	−0.17	−0.07	73.9	+0.69	+0.66	+0.03
1930	13.8	−0.67	−0.60	−0.07	11.8	+0.24	+0.23	+0.01	74.3	+0.44	+0.37	+0.06
1931	13.3	−0.54	−0.22	−0.31	12.9	+1.11	+0.89	+0.22	73.8	−0.57	−0.66	+0.09
1932	12.9	−0.38	−0.02	−0.36	13.1	+0.16	+0.12	+0.04	74.0	+0.22	−0.10	+0.32
1933	12.1	−0.77	−0.34	−0.43	12.5	−0.59	−0.49	−0.10	75.4	+1.36	+0.83	+0.53
1934	12.0	−0.11	−0.04	−0.06	11.9	−0.57	−0.40	−0.17	76.0	+0.68	+0.44	+0.23
1935	12.1	+0.04	−0.13	+0.18	11.7	−0.24	−0.20	−0.03	76.2	+0.19	+0.34	−0.15
1936	13.4	+1.29	+0.77	+0.52	11.4	−0.31	−0.22	−0.09	75.2	−0.98	−0.55	−0.43
1937	13.0	−0.37	−0.10	−0.27	11.1	−0.29	−0.23	−0.06	75.9	+0.66	+0.33	+0.34
1938	11.5	−1.46	−0.64	−0.83	11.4	+0.34	+0.28	+0.06	77.0	+1.13	+0.36	+0.77

Based on estimates in *Some Aspects of the Distribution of Income by Size* (in preparation).

column 5 of more than 2.2 percent; and in column 9 of more than 3.4 percent. Indeed, for most years absolute changes are in fractions of 1 percent. In view of the violent fluctuations during the period in total income payments and income per capita, the distribution by size as reflected by the shares of the upper income groups seems to display a marked degree of stability.

A further question immediately arises: instead of reflecting genuine changes in the distribution of income by size, may not the changes, small as they are, be due to errors and crudities in procedure and underlying data? The question is especially pertinent here since the procedure by which these income shares have been estimated involves a sequence of statistical adjustments applied to income tax returns that may well suffer from serious errors of omission and underreporting. Hence, the analysis of changes that apportions them between those that can be associated with shifts in weight *among* the several types of payment, and those due to shifts in shares of the top income groups *within* the countrywide total of each type of payment is particularly important: not only for the interest in its substantive conclusions but also for the test it provides as to whether changes can be explained in terms of data relatively independent of possible errors in tax return information.

The allocation of changes between those due to *inter*-type of payment shifts and those due to *intra*-type of payment shifts is obtained by the following simple procedure. First, multiplying the average share for 1919-38 of each type of payment received by the upper income groups (i.e., those in lines 2a-g of Table 4) by the share in each year of each type of payment in total income payments, we calculate a series that shows what the shares of the upper income groups would have been if there were shifts only in the distribution of total income payments by type and no changes in the shares of each type of payment received by the upper income groups (the *inter*-type of payment shifts series). Second, multiplying the average share for 1919-38 of each type of payment in total income payments (i.e., those in Table 4, col. 4, lines

3a-g) by the annual share of the upper income groups in each type of payment total, we obtain a series that shows what the shares of the upper income groups would have been if there were shifts only in the shares received of each type of payment and no changes in the percentage distribution of total income payments by type (the *intra*-type of payment shifts series). The two series are then adjusted so that they average out for each year to the total series of shares of the upper income groups, a very minor proportional adjustment. The year-to-year change in the total series is the arithmetic sum of the changes in the two adjusted series: the first adjusted series yielding changes associated with *inter*-type of payment shifts, the second, changes associated with *intra*-type of payment shifts.

It is clear from this brief description that the calculated *inter*-type of payment series is relatively independent of the tax returns data: of the latter it uses only the *average* percentages in lines 2a-g of Table 4 as constant weights. Hence, changes in the inter-type of payment series are produced exclusively by changes in the percentage distribution of total income payments by type; and are thus based upon estimates in *National Income and Its Composition*—estimates that are almost completely independent of tax data for individuals.

For this reason, the evidence of Table 32 that inter-type of payment shifts produce changes in shares of upper income groups (col. 3, 7, and 11) in the same direction as the total changes in them (col. 2, 6, and 10), and account for a substantial proportion of these changes, lends support to the genuineness of the latter—their independence of the vagaries of income tax data and of our procedures for treating the latter. For the shares of the upper 1 percent, changes associated with inter-type of payment shifts are in the same direction as total changes in 18 of the 19 comparisons; and account for half or more than half of the total change in 12 of these 18 (col. 2 and 3). Likewise, the changes for the 2d through 5th percentage from top and for the lower 95 percent are to a large extent accounted for by the inter-type of payment shifts. In other words, year-to-year changes in the

TABLE 33

Changes in Percentage Shares of Total Income Payments
(Current Prices) Received by Upper and Lower Income Groups
Average Values, and Differences in Rate of Movement
between Expansion and Contraction, Reference Cycles, 1919-1938
(basic variant, unadjusted for marital status and including
federal income taxes)

| | REFERENCE CYCLES | | | | | AV. FOR 5 CYCLES |
	1919-21 (1)	1921-24 (2)	1924-27 (3)	1927-32 (4)	1932-38 (5)	(6)
AVERAGE VALUE FOR EACH REFERENCE CYCLE						
Share of Upper 1%						
1 % share in total income payments	12.8	13.0	13.8	14.0	12.5	13.2
2 Change in line 1		+0.20	+0.82	+0.27	—1.57	—0.07
Change associated with shifts						
3 *Among* types of payment		—0.07	+0.42	—0.10	—0.78	—0.13
4 *Within* types of payment		+0.26	+0.40	+0.37	—0.79	+0.06
Share of 2d-5th% from Top						
5 % share in total income payments	10.4	11.2	11.4	12.1	11.8	11.4
6 Change in line 5		+0.86	+0.18	+0.69	—0.28	+0.36
Change associated with shifts						
7 *Among* types of payment		+0.61	+0.12	+0.61	—0.18	+0.29
8 *Within* types of payment		+0.24	+0.06	+0.08	—0.10	+0.07
Share of Lower 95%						
9 % share in total income payments	76.9	75.8	74.8	73.9	75.7	75.4
10 Change in line 9		—1.06	—1.00	—0.96	+1.85	—0.29
Change associated with shifts						
11 *Among* types of payment		—0.55	—0.55	—0.51	+0.96	—0.16
12 *Within* types of payment		—0.51	—0.46	—0.44	+0.90	—0.13
DIFFERENCES IN RATE OF MOVEMENT (ABSOLUTE) BETWEEN EXPANSION AND CONTRACTION						
Share of Upper 1%						
13 In share in total income payments	+1.65	+1.24	—0.05	—0.59	—1.48	+0.16
Associated with shifts						
14 *Among* types of payment	+0.84	+0.95	—0.07	—0.18	—0.67	+0.17
15 *Within* types of payment	+0.81	+0.30	+0.02	—0.41	—0.82	—0.02
Share of 2d-5th% from Top						
16 In share in total income payments	+2.59	+1.45	+0.29	+0.50	+0.74	+1.11
Associated with shifts						
17 *Among* types of payment	+1.81	+1.06	+0.21	+0.40	+0.59	+0.81
18 *Within* types of payment	+0.78	+0.39	+0.08	+0.10	+0.15	+0.30
Share of Lower 95%						
19 In share in total income payments	—4.24	—2.69	—0.24	+0.09	+0.75	—1.27
Associated with shifts						
20 *Among* types of payment	—2.65	—2.01	—0.14	—0.22	+0.08	—0.99
21 *Within* types of payment	—1.59	—0.69	—0.10	+0.31	+0.66	—0.28

shares of the upper income groups can, to a considerable extent, be explained by shifts in the relative weight of the various types of payment in the countrywide total of all income payments—an explanation that serves to reduce materially possible qualms about whether the changes may not be mere reflections of varying biases in the federal income tax data.[29]

We may now examine these short term changes more closely, keeping the distinction between those due to inter- and to intra-type of payment shifts. We study first the changes in these shares from reference cycle to reference cycle, to see whether any movements longer than those associated with reference cycles can be observed; then consider the changes from expansion to contraction within each reference cycle (Table 33).

The cycle averages in lines 1, 5, and 9 suggest that in addition to fluctuations within reference cycles there appears to have been a longer swing during the period, with a peak (or trough) in the late 1920's and a trough (or peak) in the

[29]Computations completed since this report was written show, however, that the relative size of the inter- and intra-type elements depends partly upon the period chosen as base for calculating average shares. Tables 32 and 33 use the average shares for the full period, 1919-38. Thus, in calculating the inter-type component, we derived the 1919-38 average share of the top percent of the population in each of the several types of payment, and applied these shares as weights in calculating changes due to year-to-year shifts among types of payment. Likewise, in calculating the intra-type component, we derived the 1919-38 average share of each type of payment in the countrywide aggregate of all payments, and applied these shares as weights in calculating changes due to year-to-year variations in shares of the top percent of the population in each of the several types of payment.

If instead of the average shares for 1919-38, we use as weights the given single year's shares, the division of the total change between the inter- and the intra-type components is modified substantially. On this basis, the inter-type component is still preponderant in accounting for year-to-year changes in the shares of the top 1 percent of the income population, but is not significant in the year-to-year changes in the shares of the top 2d to 5th percent. The major conclusions of Tables 32 and 33 as to the importance of inter-type shifts remain; but the relative weight of the latter is appreciably reduced, with a corresponding increase in the weight of the intra-type component.

Note to Table 33

Based on estimates in Table 32. Measures of changes within reference cycles (lines 13-21) are here on an absolute basis, i.e., they reflect absolute rises and declines (per year) in the percentage shares of the upper and lower income groups.

1930's. The annual series in Table 32 serve to confirm this impression, for the share of the upper 1 percent of the population: the peak value, reached in 1928, is followed by a long decline to a temporary trough in 1934. This longer swing is obscured in the combined share of the 2d through 5th percent from the top, although more detailed analysis might bring it out for the percents closer to the top. But the cumulated share for the upper 5 percent is still dominated by this longer swing in the upper 1 percent, which causes an inverted swing in the share of the lower 95 percent with a trough in 1928, followed by a long rise to a temporary peak in 1935. When one views the period as a whole, there seems to have been stability or a slight decline in the share of the upper 1 percent; a rise in the total share of the 2d through 5th percent from the top; and stability or a slight decline in the share of the lower 95 percent. As far as inequality in distribution of income can be reflected by the measures in Table 33, they suggest a decline in the inequality of the distribution *within* the top 5 percent group and no significant changes in shares of the top 1 or lower 95 percent.

The fluctuations within reference cycles are measured here in terms of absolute rise or decline in the percentage shares— not in percentages of average value for each cycle. This facilitates both understanding of the measures and their analysis as between inter- and intra-type of payment shifts. The evidence suggests that for the upper 1 percent of the population during the first two reference cycles shares of income declined during expansion and rose during contraction. But the pattern shifts to a reverse movement—rise in share during expansion and decline in share during contraction in the last two reference cycles. No such reversal of pattern is observed in the combined shares of the 2d through 5th percent from the top: they tend more uniformly either to decline during expansions and rise during contractions, or at least to show an algebraically greater rate of movement per year during contractions than during preceding expansions. The cumulated total for the upper 5 percent, and hence the residual share for the lower 95 percent, is still dominated by the shifting pattern of the share of the upper 1 percent. But it is clear from Table 33 that if we were to push the dividing line between upper and lower income groups further below the 5 percent break, the cumulated share of the upper group would tend to show an inverted pattern, i.e., a higher rate of movement during contractions than during expansions; and the lower group would consequently show a positive pattern. Thus, if we define inequality in the distribution of income by size in terms of the relative shares of the upper and lower income groups compared, and ask how such inequality changes during reference cycles, the answer, at least for 1919-38, would depend upon where we draw the line between the upper and lower groups. If we draw it at the 1 percent level, inequality tended to decline during expansions and to rise during contractions at the beginning of the period, and to reverse the pattern during the latter part of the period. If we were to draw the line at say 20 or 25 percent, it is plausible to infer that inequality would tend to show a pattern inverted to the reference cycle—to decline during expansions and to rise during contractions. Since the inclusion of capital gains affects chiefly the share of the upper 1 percent, merely accentuating the long term swing already indicated by Tables 32 and 33, the conclusions suggested in the text would probably hold also for the distribution by size of income inclusive of gains and losses from sale of capital assets.

The major importance of inter-type of payment shifts in accounting for the changes in the rate of movement from expansion to contraction is evident in Table 33. While both types of shifts, inter and intra, contribute to whatever total changes occur within each reference cycle, the weight of the former is on the whole markedly greater than that of the latter—a conclusion subject to the qualification stated in footnote 29 above.

The small changes in the shares in total income payments received by the top income groups may in part be due to the crudity of our estimates: were more refined measures possible, they would show somewhat greater fluctuations, tending, on the whole, to raise the magnitude of changes associated with the intra-type of payment shifts. Furthermore, the top income groups are important in determining certain categories of income use—income taxes, savings, and expenditure on some luxury and durable commodities. Minor changes in shares of total income received by the upper groups may have a substantial effect on income tax yields; on the savings-income ratio for the country; and on the proportion of income expended for certain types of consumer goods.

Finally, the estimates shed no light on the size distribution of income among lower income recipients. Yet the characteristics of that distribution are affected by an important cyclical factor—full and part time unemployment. Inequality in the distribution by size within the lower 95 or 75 percent of the population would tend to be less in expansions because the unemployed, who receive little or no income, are fewer, and greater in contractions because the unemployed are more numerous. How this cyclical fluctuation would combine with the ones suggested above, i.e., those between the upper and lower groups or within the upper group proper, to determine changes in the distribution by size through the whole range from highest to lowest is a problem that awaits further analysis.

6 Differences among Final Use Components

Inasmuch as the method used here to measure changes during business cycles involves percentages of cycle averages, it cannot be applied to net capital formation or its four components because they alternate between positive and negative values.

That cyclical fluctuations in net capital formation, no matter how measured, are wide can be seen from their effect on national income, made up as it is, of net capital formation and the flow of goods to consumers. The average decline in the rate of movement from expansion to contraction is only 12 percent in the flow of goods to consumers, while that in national income is more than one and a half times as great (Table 34, lines 1 and 2). This difference is observed in all five reference cycles; and, in relative terms, is even larger when totals in 1929 prices are compared (lines 7 and 8).

We cannot measure differences in the amplitude of changes in the components of net capital formation, but we can for

TABLE 34

National Income Categories by Type of Use
Differences in Rate of Movement between Expansion
and Contraction, Reference Cycles, 1919-1938

(all measures of change are on a per year basis and in percentages of
the average value of the series for each full reference cycle)

| | REFERENCE CYCLES | | | | | AV. FOR 5 CYCLES |
	1919-21 (1)	1921-24 (2)	1924-27 (3)	1927-32 (4)	1932-38 (5)	(6)
	CURRENT PRICES					
1 National income	—36.5	—8.5	—7.9	—24.9	—19.0	—19.4
2 Flow of goods to consumers	—26.7	0.0	—4.7	—17.8	—8.5	—11.6
3 Perishable	—30.7	+1.4	—7.5	—17.3	—15.0	—13.8
4 Semidurable	—35.6	—13.9	—3.3	—19.6	—8.0	—16.1
5 Consumer durable	—34.9	—15.3	—12.9	—31.8	—39.1	—26.8
6 Services	—12.8	+9.6	+0.2	—14.0	+5.9	—2.2
	1929 PRICES					
7 National income	—8.2	—8.7	—3.5	—18.2	—12.9	—10.3
8 Flow of goods to consumers	—0.8	0.0	—0.4	—10.3	—4.1	—3.1
9 Perishable	—1.0	+4.2	+0.2	—4.8	—5.5	—1.4
10 Semidurable	+32.6	—18.7	+7.3	—9.8	+0.2	+2.3
11 Consumer durable	—18.4	—18.2	—16.3	—24.6	—35.1	—22.5
12 Services	—8.7	+8.2	+1.1	—12.2	+3.2	—1.7

Based on estimates in *National Product since 1869,* Table I 18, col. 3, Table I 19, col. 3, and Table I 5.

the four components of the flow of goods to consumers, in both current and 1929 prices. Totals in current prices show the expected differences: widest amplitude in consumer durables and narrowest in the services category. Also, while the rate of movement of consumer durables and semidurables declines from expansion to contraction in all five reference cycles, perishables do not in one, and services do not in three.

Adjustment to constant prices narrows the amplitude of changes in all four categories and increases the number of cycles during which there is no decline in the rate of movement from expansion to contraction—in perishable to two, and in semidurable to three. Consumer durables, in which price changes are smallest, are influenced least by the price adjustment. Consequently, on the average and in all five reference cycles, their rate of movement from expansion to contraction still declines sharply. The average for perishable commodities drops to one-tenth of its level for totals in current prices. The large positive entry for the flow of semidurable commodities in the 1919-21 cycle causes its average for the period to be positive rather than negative. The effect of the price adjustment on the measures for the services category is not as great, owing, as in the case of durable commodities, to the temporal rigidity of prices. But the narrow amplitude of changes during business cycles characteristic of values in current prices is accentuated.

Despite possible errors attaching to the allocation of the flow of goods to consumers among its four categories, and especially to the adjustment for price changes, the main differences in Table 34 between the estimates in current and constant prices and among the categories are beyond reasonable doubt. The greater responsiveness to business cycles of flows in current prices than of those in constant prices, and the wider amplitude of changes in the flow of consumer durable commodities and the narrower of those in the flow of other categories are confirmed by other data and easily accounted for.

The relative (and for averages, even absolute) dispersion among the categories of final use in the amplitude of changes during business cycles is greater for values in constant prices than for those in current prices: for the latter the average is —11.6, with a range from —2.2 to —26.8, for the former, —3.1, with a range from +2.3 to —22.5 (col. 6). Thus, just as in our comparison of the inter-industry dispersion of net income (current prices) and employment, so also here the tendency toward covariation in prices imposes an element of uniformity on changes during business cycles in the several consumer goods categories in current prices that is absent when they are measured in constant prices.

In this brief account of short term fluctuations in national income and its components, only the amplitude of participation in business cycles could be measured. Differences in such amplitude were established among net income originating in different industries; various types of income or income payment; shares of upper and lower income groups; components by type of use; volumes in current and in constant prices. These confirmed expectations based upon already established knowledge of differences among economic processes in their participation in business cycles.

That the comprehensive totals of national income and of its components are so clearly responsive to business cycles and that the differences suggested by studies based upon partial data are confirmed and extended in the analysis of the wider components lends firmness to notions concerning the pervasiveness of business cycles; and the importance in them of differences in response on the part of different processes. Obviously, differences in response among the several processes, all of which are inter-related in the economic system, help us to understand not only how a cyclical expansion or contraction, once generated, spreads, but also how it comes to an end because of the braking influence of the least responsive processes upon those that respond and fluctuate widely. Likewise, knowledge of these differences is clearly relevant to social policy directed at ameliorating the effects of business cycles or at reducing their incidence. It would be natural for such social policy to address its measures in the first order to the sectors of the economy that respond most violently and, regardless of their possibly strategic role in the cyclical process, experience its undesirable consequences most acutely.

National income measures can contribute to the understanding and control of business cycles much more than the brief analysis above suggests. Annual estimates are available for many more aspects of the performance of the economy than could be discussed above; and for recent years quarterly and monthly measures have become accessible, although so far for too short a period to warrant analysis. Yet it must always be remembered that we deal here with summaries that conceal a variety of experience and fail to reveal the mechanism of response of the individual, firm, or single institution. The proper cognizance of all these is indispensable to both theoretical understanding and policy formulation. The apparent simplicity of the picture portrayed by estimates of national income and its components should not free us from the responsibility of studying the behavior of the groups of individuals and firms whose activities are merged in these over-all totals; and of paying due attention to the variety of their experience in any consideration of business cycle policy.

PART IV

Problems of Interpretation

Before national income estimates can be interpreted properly, (a) the basic assumptions underlying them, (b) their statistical accuracy, (c) the significance of their levels, trends, and short term variations must be scrutinized. Under (a) are questions concerning the scope of activities whose results are included in national income; the distinction between their gross and net product; the basis upon which products of various description are evaluated and added; the boundaries of the nation in the definition of 'national' income; and the like. Under (b) are questions concerning the statistical approach, the character of the primary or derived data, the validity of the procedures used to approximate sectors for which data are lacking, the margin of error in the final estimates. Under (c) are the numerous questions that arise when we try to interpret the evidence of national income estimates in the light of other knowledge or processes and interrelations in the economy; the relations between changes in national income totals, their components, and other aspects of the economic system; the causes of the levels or changes, i.e, their association with factors whose effects are known from information other than national income data proper; and so on.

These three groups of questions have so far been commented upon only casually, and obviously cannot be analyzed adequately here. In choosing the few that can be, we omit questions under (b) and (c). The former cannot be discussed effectively except with the help of extensive notes and tables; and the interested student should turn to the publications containing the detailed descriptions of sources and procedures, most of which are cited in the tables or footnotes above. Questions under (c) can hardly be analyzed properly, except

111

in studies of some specific problem, where estimates of national income and its components are one of several bodies of relevant data. It is, therefore, impossible here to go beyond the tentative suggestions advanced above in discussing what estimates of national income show concerning its structure, long term trends, and short term changes.

Even of the questions under (a), only those are treated that seem to bear most directly upon a proper understanding of the meaning of national income estimates. Other problems are noted, but not discussed; still others are not even mentioned.

1   The Distinction between Net and Gross

In computing a national income total for a year, we count the products turned out, the resources put in, or the monetary counterparts of either. In such a count, a major problem is to avoid duplication. If we add commodities and services, it would obviously be duplication to include both the value of coal produced and the value of the commodity produced in consuming the coal. If we add input of resources, it would obviously be duplication to include the input of both the machine and the labor expended on its repair or replacement. If we add monetary counterparts, in the form of payments for products or resources, it would obviously be duplication to include both payments by consumers for butter and payments by butter producers to farmers for cream. National income is net in that no duplication of this kind inflates the total, so far as it can be avoided. Any total inflated by duplication is qualified as 'gross'. The distinction between net and gross hinges then upon how duplication is avoided.

The simplicity of the examples cited may mislead us into thinking that the problem could be easily resolved by applying the test of physical disappearance. We consider it duplication to include both cream and butter, because cream has physically vanished or, rather, assumed the form of butter. Hence, we could presumably avoid duplication if in adding products turned out during the year, we excluded those consumed in the production process, i. e., the ones that lost their physical identity and became embodied, as it were, in products that were *not* so consumed.

But how shall we (a) define the production process, and (b) treat items that apparently remain unchanged, yet are said to be consumed in the production process?

a) Is the loss of the physical identity of butter consumed in the household by the wage earner and his family, and its embodiment in the health and efficiency of present and future workers consumption in the production process? Is the maintenance and increase of the country's population and of its efficiency a productive process similar to that of turning out steel or perfume? If so, we must, to avoid duplication, exclude from the total of commodities and services turned out during the year not only those consumed in producing other goods but also all those consumed in the household in maintaining and increasing the country's productive population and its efficiency; but include the value of that increase. Or do we consider consumption in households part of life in general rather than a production process, and the supply of goods to households a primary purpose of economic activity to which the latter is subordinate? If so, we must classify consumption in households as *ultimate,* consumption in the production process as *intermediate,* and include in national income the full value of goods flowing to households, even though most of them lose their physical identity.

b) In practice, consumption in the production process is allowed for even when physical destruction is not evident; e. g., for durable capital items such as a building or a machine. While some instruments have been devised to record the rate of physical destruction for long lived equipment, depreciation is based less on any observed physical deterioration than on an assumption of economic loss. Technical progress, changes in tastes, etc., tend to make equipment obsolescent before it is worn out.

The test of physical destruction or transformation in the production process does not, therefore, automatically resolve the problem of avoiding duplication in measuring national income. Of the two problems its application raises, outlined above under (a) and (b), we discuss solely the first in the light of the goals of economic activity and the consequent distinction between ultimate and intermediate consumption (or a parallel pair of concepts, final and intermediate goods).

As we have just seen, if no ultimate goal is set to economic activity—except mere increase in the supply of goods—all consumption becomes part of the production process; to eliminate duplication, all goods consumed during the year are excluded, and national income equals the value of net additions to the population and its efficiency plus the value of net additions to stocks of commodities or of claims against foreign countries. But if we assume that the primary objective of economic activity is to provide goods to satisfy wants of the members of the nation; that national income is for man and not man for the increase of the country's capacity and national income, then ultimate consumption can be defined as the use of goods in direct fulfilment of this primary objective and measured as the sum *at full value* of all goods placed at the disposal of ultimate consumers during the year; plus such changes in the stock of intermediate goods as affect the future supply of goods to consumers—*net* changes in the stock of all commodities (outside households) and of claims against foreign countries.

This is the widely accepted definition of national income. It rests upon the basic assumption that to provide goods to consumers is the primary purpose of economic activity. It recognizes as duplication the inclusion of goods consumed in the production process alone; and defines the production process to exclude the goods consumed in maintaining the inhabitants and enabling them to grow and multiply. It includes the *gross* value of the flow of goods to ultimate consumers and the *net* value of changes in the stock of capital goods.

If the recognition of a consumption process as representing the satisfaction of an ultimate goal of economic activity permits inclusion of goods so consumed in national income, recognizing other ultimate goals would lead to a larger total. Indeed, one could argue that at some periods other purposes of economic activity emerge; e.g., provision of weapons for military conflict in time of war. If it is recognized as another primary goal, the gross value of war output must be included in national income, which would then exceed that estimated by treating war output as a species of capital formation (subordinate to the basic aim of providing goods to consumers) and therefore including only the net change in inventories of war goods.[30]

The basic assumption concerning goals of economic activity can thus range from recognizing none except sheer increase of capacity as measured by population and capital—national income for national income's sake—to recognizing several so that the flow of several categories of products is taken at their gross value (goods to ultimate consumers, goods for the armed conflict, certain categories of public or private capital). With these variations in basic assumptions, national income would vary.

Yet, though different basic assumptions are justified for some exceptional short periods, e.g., during a major war, that underlying the customary definition of national income can be defended as the sole valid one in the longer run, on either or both of two grounds. The first is the unique relevance of satisfying men's wants to national income as an *appraisal* notion. National income is not a measure of activity, of how much effort, toil, and trouble economic activity represents; but of its contribution, of its success in attaining its goal. Viewed in this light, there is no other long standing purpose except to provide the material means with which wants of the members of society, present and future, can be satisfied.

Second, the entire pattern of economic organization in modern society seems to have the provision of goods to consumers as its primary goal. The concern various social institutions manifest for maintaining and increasing the flow of goods to its members, and the subordination of other goals to that end cannot be demonstrated statistically, but is an impression conveyed by measures taken to ensure this primary goal and to overcome any serious obstacles to its attainment. At any rate, it is difficult to formulate a different goal of

[30]For a more detailed discussion and statistical illustration of this point see *National Product in Wartime*, Part I.

economic activity of equally primary importance for most nations in the last century and a half.[31]

Yet, in taking this position, we should consider one possible qualification. While provision of goods to consumers may be recognized as the primary goal of economic activity, and hence the flow of such goods treated as ultimate rather than intermediate consumption, is all of it wanted by consumers *qua* consumers? Is not some of it wanted by consumers in their capacity as producers? That part would represent an occupational expense—intermediate rather than ultimate consumption. If a man spends a portion of his income on bus fares to travel to and from work, are bus services a flow of goods to him as an ultimate consumer? What about education preparing individuals for their occupations, or the demand for certain goods for living at a level that facilitates the individual's success as a producer?

Unquestionably, in our industrial, urban civilization many items of ultimate consumption are chosen for the sake of productive efficiency, and could be classified as intermediate rather than ultimate consumption. But the distinction is tenuous; and carrying it too far would bring us right back to denying the possibility of ultimate consumption altogether. For if education is conceived simply as preparation for livelihood and

[31]If one entertains a social philosophy in which the criteria of economic activity are other than the satisfaction of consumers' wants (e.g., the test of contributing to the military glory of the state or the honor of the nation couched in terms of blood and soil) one would not accept the provision of goods to consumers as the primary goal. Likewise, if one's view of economic institutions leads to the conclusion that they, in fact, are not organized for the purpose of enhancing the material welfare of consumers, the second ground for accepting the latter as the primary goal in defining national income is absent. In these cases, another definition of national income is called for; and another total, if the concept is at all measurable, would result.

This has distinct bearing upon international comparisons of national income, when made for economies differing widely in the character of their social organization and goals; or for inter-temporal comparisons for one and the same country when the character of social organization and goals have altered radically. In such cases, the application of the customary definition of national product means, in fact, applying criteria that may be relevant to one term of the comparison but not to the other. Even so, there may be significance in judging the net contribution of two or more national economies by the criteria recognized by one alone.

not as the enhancement of living, and if a man's residence and its appurtenances are counted simply as the domestic equipment appropriate for the production of his income, then, since the satisfactions of the consumer are inextricably bound up in the circle of means and ends with the needs of the producer, the whole category of ultimate consumption disappears. As long as we recognize the latter as the purpose of society, we must avoid overstressing the occupational orientation that may be present in some degree in this or the other sector of the flow of goods to consumers. While the flow of goods to consumers is inflated in that it includes some intermediate consumption in addition to ultimate, the 'grossness' of the flow, and of the national product total of which it is the preponderant part, is limited.

2 Why Gross National Product?

If we accept the definition of national income just discussed, the total is net only in the sense that all consumption of intermediate goods is subtracted, not in that *all* consumption is subtracted. Totals that may be termed 'gross' differ from net in that they are gross of some intermediate consumption, in that there is deliberate duplication in including both the value of the final products and of some intermediate goods consumed in turning them out. The reason is that these gross totals may be useful as measures of activity, for national income measures net product or contribution alone.

This difference in purpose may be illustrated by 'gross national product', as defined and estimated in the National Bureau's studies of capital formation, and 'gross national product at market prices', as defined and estimated by the Department of Commerce. The former does not deduct the current consumption of durable capital, such as buildings or producers' equipment. Gross of that consumption, it exceeds national income by that amount. The reason for this deliberate duplication is that, in practice, the distinction between the need for durable capital for replacement and the demand for durable capital for additions is quite tenuous, in the *short* run. Within a relatively short period, the capacity of an item of durable equipment is elastic; and in few, if any, items does physical deterioration compel replacement, leaving no discretion to the entrepreneur. If, therefore, we wish to understand short term variations in the flow of durable capital, we should measure it gross rather than net, since short term decisions, whether of private or public entrepreneurs, are more likely to be in terms of replacement and additional demand combined than between capital for replacement and capital for new additions. Likewise, the effect of entrepreneurial decisions on short term variations in volume of activity is clearer when we deal with a total that includes its determining component, i.e., gross rather than net capital formation.

The Department of Commerce's 'gross national product at market prices' is gross in that it does not allow for the consumption of durable capital in private hands; or for the part of government expenditures that represents depreciation on government owned durable capital goods or the value of services contributed by government to private enterprises and consumed by the latter in the production process. Thus, while at the final product level, national income or net national product is the sum of the flow of goods to consumers and net capital formation, and our gross national product is the sum of the flow of goods to consumers and gross capital formation, the Department of Commerce's gross national product at market prices is the sum of (a) the flow of goods to consumers, minus government services to consumers, (b) gross capital formation under private auspices, and (c) all government expenditures for commodities and services.

As indicated in *National Product in Wartime* (App. I) the essential reason for a total in which both private capital formation and government activities are taken gross lies in the usefulness, for the study of short term changes, of measuring both the demand for capital by private enterprises and government activities in terms of gross capital formation and total government expenditures. If we conceive the demand for capital by private enterprises and total government activity as two independent variables whose short term variations generate changes in aggregate economic activity, then both private capital formation and government activity should be treated **gross**. And the over-all measure of activity must also include both gross private capital formation and total government expenditures, since what is in the part must also be in the whole.

This orientation of the concept to the importance, as independent variables in short term changes, of the demand for capital by private enterprises and government expenditures is evident in the basic classification of the Department's gross national product at market prices. The three main components are consumers' outlay, private gross capital formation, total expenditures by government on goods (i.e., excluding pure transfer transactions). Of these three, the last two are considered variables subject to wide, independent changes in the short run. Government expenditures especially tend to be treated as a variable that can be affected by direct action much more easily than the passive though larger consumers' outlay, and the volatile but relatively uncontrollable private capital formation.[32]

Many other gross totals could be calculated by segregating other sectors in the economy deemed sufficiently strategic for their activity to be conceived as an independent variable whose short term changes affect the activity of the economy at large. If we were to assume, for example, that agriculture is a sector that could be so classified, we would get a national total gross of the consumption of durable capital and of products of other industries by agriculture. The share of agriculture

[32]In addition to the use of the concept in discussion of postwar problems, an earlier use of the Department of Commerce's gross national product at market prices was in connection with the analysis of government policy in war years. War demands were estimated in terms of war production and outlay programs, at gross value. Government policy with reference to the private sector could be formulated and implemented more easily in terms of gross than of net capital formation, and of consumers' outlay than of flow of goods to consumers (which includes direct tax payments as the measure of government services to individuals). Hence, for the purpose of analyzing the proximate effects of government policy in war years, a sum of these three gross components was more useful than the more abstruse (if in the longer run, more meaningful) net national product.

Consequently, a happier name for the Department's gross total might perhaps be 'total expenditures', since it represents a sum of outlays by individuals, by private enterprises (on capital), and by governments.

would then equal agricultural expenditures on all commodities and services (including those of independent farmers) instead of the net difference between total value product and the value of materials, semifabricates, durable equipment, and services of other industries consumed in its production. The usefulness of each of the many gross national products that could be defined and measured in this way lies in the validity of the assumption that the sectors selected as strategic and best understood in terms of their gross activity are indeed determinants of changes in total output and better studied in terms of gross than of net national product.

It would take us too far afield to appraise the validity of selecting this or that area for 'gross' treatment, whether as implied in the gross totals already discussed or in others that might be devised. But two comments are appropriate here. First, as we increase the number of sectors in the economy that can be distinguished and that, conceived in terms of their gross activity, are determinants of levels and changes in national product or foci of public policy, the gross national total becomes larger and larger since the duplication is correspondingly widened. The culmination of duplication as more and more sectors of the economy are recognized as determinants may make the grossest national total the sum of the expenditures (or intake) of each single producing enterprise in the country. Such a total would naturally be vastly larger than any gross total calculated so far; and many times that of national income.

Second, we reiterate that any gross total, precisely because it is gross, contains some duplication and inflation, and should not be confused with a net product such as national income. It is the latter that attempts to gauge the net result of economic activity, and it is its size and fluctuations that are the chief criteria in judging the success with which the economy functions. There may and possibly should be a legion of gross totals, reflecting different approaches to the ways different sectors of activity affect or can be made to affect the net product. They are auxiliary and subsidiary concepts needed to build up the chain of cause-effect relations that determine the net end product, and useful as steps in technical analysis intended to bring out the proximate causes of failure or success. Regardless of technicians' interest in gross totals, society at large is interested primarily in national income, provided the implicit basic assumptions as to goals reflect its general views concerning what economic activity is for. Large gross totals do not necessarily ensure satisfactory levels and composition of the net product. Given the latter, there is little reason to worry about the levels and composition of any gross total.

3 National Income and Welfare

Do estimates of national income measure the net contribution of economic activity to its primary goal—provision of goods to individuals—without errors of commission and omission? Do all commodities and services ordinarily included contribute to the satisfaction of consumers' wants, present or future? Are all the goods, i.e., all the sources of satisfying consumers' wants, made available in any year included in national income as estimated in this country today? We consider first the possible errors of commission, then those of omission.

Things desirable in the eyes of one individual may be matters of indifference to the group of which he is a member, or even considered deleterious by many; and things wanted by the majority may be frowned upon by the minority. In determining what are goods from the viewpoint of satisfying consumers' wants, we cannot assign both positive and negative signs to those wanted by some but deemed pernicious by others, then strike algebraic balances. Rather we must decide what, on the whole, are goods and should be included. In the statistical measurement of national income the question reduces itself to what commodities and services should be excluded because, by and large, they do not contribute to the goal of economic activity—satisfaction of consumers' wants. Specific examples may range from services, such as are rendered Mr. Smith by a professional gang of killers in disposing of his rival Mr. Jones, to commodities, such as harmful drugs or useless patent medicines.

If in such a classification needs and relevance to needs were defined in terms of an imagined application of scientific knowledge and broad principles of ethics, we would exclude from national income many commodities and services now included. Many foods and drugs are worthless by scientific standards of nutrition and medication; many household appurtenances are irrelevant to any scientifically established needs for shelter and comfort; many service activities as well as commodities are desired for the sake of impressing foreigners or our fellow countrymen and could hardly measure up to ethical principles of behavior in relation to the rest of mankind. National income, as estimated here, is subject to errors of commission in that it includes commodities and services that are not goods, i.e., do not contribute to the satisfaction of needs, *if* the criteria are scientific standards and broad canons of ethics.

It would be instructive to estimate national income as the sum of products that are unequivocally sources of satisfying needs objectively determined from the viewpoint of mankind as a whole. The estimate could be described as a given nation's share in the world's current new supply of 'approved' goods. Such estimates would aid national groups in appraising their social activities in general and their economic performance in particular. But they would not be what national income estimates as customarily prepared are designed to be—measures of the contribution of the nation's economy to satisfying the wants society recognizes as legitimate.

We exclude all illegal commodities or services, e.g., hired murder and the manufacture and sale of illegal drugs, as far as we can with the inadequate statistical data at hand. We include commodities and services not prohibited as long as they find a buyer (presumably they would not exist without one), though they may not be useful from any objective standpoint. In short, in the absence of society's explicit declaration to the contrary, the wants of the individual buyer are the criterion. Erratic the test of legality may be (consider the prohibition years) and difficult of application to certain activities (consider a shady business deal that has not as yet been prosecuted in courts and may never be), but it is the only one at the disposal of a national income estimator unless he sets himself up as a social philosopher and decides to ignore the consensus of society as to what are not goods, i.e., not positive contributions to the approved ends of economic activity.

There are of course numerous payments and transactions that do not represent a commodity produced or a service rendered: and whenever national income is estimated from payments (rather than from the value of commodities and services), such transfers also are omitted; e.g., gambling gains, net gains on sales of capital assets without any preceding input of resources to account for the gain, and gifts. All these transfers among individuals may greatly affect the eventual shares various members of society receive of the current net product; but they do not directly determine its size, if it is defined as the net value of commodities and services produced during the year. The distinction between transfer payments and payments that are evidence of real production is scarcely so simple, but this is another of those problems we can no more than mention.[33]

Judged in the light of all possible ways of satisfying consumers' wants, national income as customarily measured is subject to larger errors of omission than of commission. Errors of omission arise, first, from the deliberate restriction of national income to the net product of *economic* activity proper, and hence the deliberate exclusion of activities that may satisfy wants but are not economic. Even within the area of economic activities proper, especially if broadly defined, national income estimates omit some types of product. Finally, by definition, they neglect completely any consideration of such costs of economic activity as impinge directly upon consumers' satisfaction or the welfare of the community.

Life is full of activities that lead to the satisfaction of consumers' needs and hence their welfare, only some of which can be classified as economic. In extreme cases the distinction is easy. Taking a pleasant walk or playing a game of chess with a friend satisfies certain wants, but is not an

[33]In actual measurement, transfers are sometimes included; but only because the production sources from which they arise cannot be measured directly. An illustration is the inclusion of relief payments by governments in totals that have government savings as an offsetting item.

economic activity; working in a factory or an office is. But what about the household services performed by the housewife and other members of the family? What about cultivating one's own vegetable garden?

It has become customary to base the distinction between economic and noneconomic activities on the closeness of ties with the market. Every pursuit whose products are either sold on the market or are largely directed toward it is treated as economic; no others are, though their yield in the way of satisfying wants may be substantial. This solution has a great advantage in that it segregates the sector of life concerned largely with economic activities, and in which measurement is feasible because the yardstick (no matter how it may have to be adjusted) is the market price. In a highly developed economy the disadvantages are reduced by the fact that the majority of the activities intended to produce goods for consumers are market-bound. Even so, the magnitudes omitted are far from minor. For example, the value of housewives' services are roughly estimated at some $23 billion in 1929, or more than one-fourth of national income.[34] And in countries where the market is less developed than in the United States, the limitation of economic activities to those market-bound leads to a major undercount.

The national income estimator must choose between comprehensive definition—with the consequence that large sectors of the economy either cannot be measured on a continuous basis or cannot be included with more precisely measurable sectors because the errors are so enormous—and a narrower definition that confines economic activities to those market-bound— for which tolerably reliable estimates can be made. In current national income measurement in this country, the decision is usually in favor of the second alternative. And it finds support in the argument that the activities so segregated for measurement are the ones subject primarily to economic criteria and rationale; whereas those that are not directed at the market are much more a part of life in general. One may

[34]See *National Income and Its Composition*, Vol. Two, p. 433.

and does discharge a housekeeper for inefficiency in managing a household, but by itself this is rarely a ground for divorce.

However justified, this limitation results in omitting a substantial group of activities important in satisfying the needs and wants of the members of society. Moreover, some market-bound activities are omitted largely because they cannot be measured on a continuous basis—taking boarders or lodgers, spare-time jobs, and the like. In coverage, a continuous national income series is thus always on the short side even in terms of market-bound activities, which it tends to omit if they are casual and hence elusive of measurement.[35]

The national income estimator cannot do much about such omissions, since scarcity or lack of data is inherent in the nature of the omitted areas. But in interpreting national income movements in terms of satisfying consumers' wants, the limitation of national income largely to noncasual market-bound activities must be stressed. In this country as in many others where the market is always being extended, the relative importance of the household as a source of consumer goods is declining. Many activities formerly performed by the housewife or other members of the family and not measured (baking, sewing, canning, etc.) have progressively been taken over by business enterprises and gone into market-bound activities; other household functions have vanished without leaving a direct substitute in business activity. Hence, national income totals tend to exaggerate the upward movement in the supply of goods to consumers, if such supply is comprehensively defined as coming from both market-bound and family activities. Likewise, a comparison of the national income of two countries at different stages of the commercialization of family production must take into account the differing importance of the market sphere in the total provision of goods to consumers. The omission of casual activities also imparts an upward bias to the secular trend of national income, since their importance relative to those covered diminishes as more people move to cities and engage in regular, full time, pursuits.

[35]For estimates of the magnitudes see, for example, *ibid.*, pp. 419-35.

The effect on the interpretation of short term changes in national income is at least as great. During any expansion, whether associated with business cycles or with wars, people move from nonmarket to market areas and from occasional to full time jobs; and in the larger net product the proportion of measurable market-bound activities increases at the expense of nonmarket activities or occasional jobs. As many of us are all too aware, during recent years, when the pressure of war needs for the expansion of market-bound production was especially intense, the number of persons available for family household work decreased materially. *Total* net production, including production within the household, increased much less than production on farms, in factories, shops, and offices. During short term contractions, on the contrary, the shrinkage of the market sphere swells the number of persons available for services both within the household and for casual jobs. Being confined to noncasual market-bound activities, national income is thus a more cyclically sensitive index than a more comprehensive total that would include the large productive sector of the household as well as occasional jobs and pursuits. Variations in it therefore exaggerate short term changes in the more comprehensive total.

We come finally to what some may consider the gravest omission—the deliberate exclusion of the human cost of turning out the net product; i.e., such disadvantages as are concomitants of acquiring an income and cramp the recipients' (and others') style as a consumer. One example would be long working hours. If to turn out a net product of a given size requires a work week that leaves little time for leisure, the producers cannot derive much satisfaction as consumers, i.e., as individuals who have certain wants and preferences. Another example would be the strain some jobs impose. If by and large a task is disagreeable, exhausting, dull, monotonous, or nerve wracking, the cost to the producer as a consumer is higher than when the task is light, instructive, diversified, or amusing. The range of illustrations is wide—from these obvious ones to more tenuous allegations concerning the costs of unpleasant features of the business-urban civilization such as blatant advertising and the ruthless despoiling and defacing of the country-side.

National income is not intended to measure such costs. It gauges the net positive contribution to consumers' satisfaction in the form of commodities and services; the burden of work and discomfort are ignored. And it may well be questioned whether such costs are measurable; or if measurable, could be estimated in terms comparable to those in which net product is estimated. Nor is it easy to say whether the long term trends or short term fluctuations in these costs parallel those in net product or are in opposite directions. Some of these trends are clear. Working hours have been progressively shortened, and many of the heavier jobs, demanding stamina and endurance, are now performed by machinery. On the other hand, it is claimed that the monotony and dissatisfaction to the individual as an individual due to greater specialization and the repetition of a few motions have increased, and that so has the nervous tension. The balance of such claims and counterclaims cannot be struck.

The reason for calling attention to this aspect of economic activity, completely neglected in national income measurement, is its possible contribution toward understanding some of the longer term trends. It warns us against too easy an acceptance of the thesis that a high national income is the sole desideratum in theory or the dominant motive in fact in a nation's economy. The reduction in working hours, the decisions made by countries that discourage as rapid a growth of population and of national product as could be attained (consider immigration restrictions); the willingness of some business men to adopt a policy of live and let live when they might expect a greater net return from vigorous and aggressive competition; the emphasis some individuals put on the importance of other than economic incentives proper—are all indications that both in society at large and among the groups and individuals it comprises definite limits are set upon a maximum net product as measured in national income. Both recently and in the past a potentially larger net national product has been forfeited for the sake of mitigating some intangible costs of the type illustrated above. Though unable to measure them, we must recognize that their omission renders national income merely one element in the evaluation of the net welfare assignable to the nation's economic activity.

4 Consistent Valuation

After we agree upon what to include in national income and what to exclude, the next task is to find a common denominator for the various goods so that we can add them. The thousands of commodities and services must be converted into homogeneous values and added before we can study changes in them from year to year or the shares of various sectors for a given year. The problems that arise in the attempt to devise such a common denominator are perhaps more intricate than any discussed so far: in them inhere all the questions of inclusion and exclusion, but in the more difficult form of assigning quantitative weights (which can range from zero to very large numbers) rather than just marking the items by a plus (to be included) or by a minus (to be excluded).

If the various items included could be measured in terms of some physical property by precise instruments, and if we could agree that the estimates reflect consistently (across time and space) the economic significance of the items, valuation would be easy. But neither *if* is valid. It is in fact impossible to measure the physical properties of the full contents of national income, for the simple reason that some parts have no recognizable physical identity. Thus, even on the most tangible level, i.e., product, national income includes such items as *net* construction or *net* flow of producers' equipment, which are not congeries of physically identifiable buildings or machinery. Moreover, no imaginable physical property of goods could be accepted as in any way reflecting consistently their economic significance, i.e., their importance in terms of costs and returns.

Another simple way to deal with the problem would be to accept market prices at their face value. One good reason for confining national income to products of market-bound activities is the availability of market prices, which surely approximate the relative economic significance of various goods more closely than any physical property. If we could assume further that market prices reflect the relative economic significance of different categories of goods consistently as between two years or within the same year among distinctly different types of market, consistent, that is, with the input of real resources such as labor and the satisfaction consumers derive from the product, the problem would vanish. All we would have to do would be to find market prices for any given year, weight the various items that enter national income, and add.

The problem exists precisely because market prices are not consistent from period to period, and at a given point of time in different types of market. Prices of a physically identical commodity change from year to year. Even if the change is due to shifts in real costs or tastes, not to a general price inflation or deflation, we cannot use changing price totals and derive a comparable national income series. We still have to use prices at some point of time, i.e., the weights expressing the relative economic significance in a fixed base period. But most price changes over time are due to the general imperfections of our money mechanisms which create widespread movements in the price level. And society itself acknowledges this defect in trying to improve the mechanism and to curb the more extreme variations or trends.

Nor are market prices a consistent valuation base at a point of time. For example, a surgeon charges his private patient $1,000 for an operation he performs free in the hospital clinic. Such differentials in prices of physically identical commodities and services abound. While they may correspond to differences in the value of the monetary unit to would-be purchasers, a fixed base is as essential for different categories of goods as for changes over time.

These two aspects of the valuation problem—changes over time and differences in pricing bases among several sectors of the economy at a given time—are distinct. Treated differently in the historical development of quantitative economics and of national income measurement, they are kept separate even in the brief discussion below.

The problem of adjusting for changes in prices over time
has long been recognized; and the availability of series for
many groups of commodities has facilitated statistical solutions.
Though difficult questions remain, their character is well
known. All we need stress here is that to adjust national
income for temporal changes in prices is far more difficult
than to adjust any one component. Because of the very com-
prehensiveness of national income totals, they cannot be estimated directly in terms of quantities, then weighted by some
constant prices; and the 'deflation' of the current price totals
for changes in prices over time requires price indexes of a com-
prehensiveness virtually impossible. It is difficult enough to
get comparable prices for groups of commodities fairly
standardized in quality, such as steel or cotton of specific
grades. But when one visualizes the variety of goods included
in national income, and the importance in it of services or commodities subject to rapid qualitative changes, the difficulty of
'deflating' the current dollar totals precisely seems insur-
mountable. National income totals in constant prices are consequently rough approximations, though always measuring net
product more accurately than unadjusted totals in current
prices.

Although the second aspect of the problem—the differentials in price bases among the various sectors of the economy
—has also long been recognized, few statistical attempts have
been made to solve it, chiefly for lack of proper data—prices
of identical goods in different markets; e.g., prices of meat of
the same grade to consumers in lower and higher income neigh-
borhoods; or prices for an identical service paid by governments and by corporations. Rich though our price data are,
comparison is possible for merely a few items. Precisely because of the different characteristics of markets, the share of
common, identical goods is likely to be small in each, and that
of different (though comparable) goods large; hence, for just
the categories for which price differentials may be large, prices
cannot be compared except through analytical experiments designed to render two qualitatively different goods truly comparable.

Whatever the reason, national income totals, even in constant prices, are not adjusted for differences in price bases of the component sectors. Consequently, the weights assigned components at any given period may be affected by differences in price bases; i.e., the components would be weighted differently were an attempt made to put them on a comparable price basis. And whenever the relative weights of components characterized by different price bases change materially, the movements of national income in constant prices are also affected.[36]

The far reaching effects of this failure to adjust for differences in price bases may be illustrated by the perennial bundle of problems arising in measuring the share of government.[37] Unlike business enterprises and individuals, governments sell most of their services on a compulsory basis—setting the volume, composition, and price by legislative fiat. On the buying side too, governments are not subject to the same rules as private firms or individuals, incurring deficits without the economic penalties attached to them in the world of private enterprise. Government is not unique in this respect—some public utilities also exercise compulsion in their selling and are likewise, for brief periods, immune to the fateful consequences of deficits. But the far higher degree to which government possesses these peculiarities than any other sector of the economy puts several stumbling blocks in the way of national income measurement. First, to differentiate between intermediate and final products of government activity is exceedingly difficult. Were enterprises free to buy and pay for government services as they do coal or services of legal firms, their payments could be considered the value of intermediate services rendered by government. But the government exacts a compulsory price in the form of taxes; and in the organization and accounting of its activities does not separate services to enterprises from those to ultimate consumers. Likewise, were

[36]See the effect of the attempt to adjust for such price differentials between the war and the nonwar sectors in recent years in *National Product in Wartime*, Part II.

[37]Some of these could be more appropriately discussed in other sections; e.g., in connection with the distinction between net and gross. But it seemed best to note the whole array of questions at one place in the discussion.

individuals free to buy and pay for services of governments as they do those of physicians or of domestic servants, their payments could be considered the value of the final product of government activity. But the element of compulsion and the difficulty of a functional classification of government activity exists here also.

Second, are the prices paid by government for productive factors engaged under its auspices similar to those paid by business firms to their employees, capital, etc.? Third, should the government be treated like a corporation, and its undistributed profits and losses considered compensation to the factor of enterprise engaged in the government 'industry'?

The mode of settling these various problems will affect the size of national income, its composition, and changes in it over time. As a greater or smaller allowance is made for intermediate services of government, there is a greater or smaller allowance for duplication, with corresponding effects on national income as a net total. If we adjust for the differences between the prices government and business firms pay for the things they buy, we will get one national income total; if we do not, another. If we recognize the validity of the concept of net government savings, national income will be larger when the savings are positive and smaller when the savings are negative. And there will be corresponding effects on the share of government in national income, as well as on temporal changes in both.

The arbitrary solutions given these questions in the national income estimates prepared at the National Bureau in recent years were, in our judgment, the least unsatisfactory for what is essentially an insoluble problem. It was thought that because of the joint character of most government activities (e.g., national defense, provision of justice), services by government to business enterprises cannot be differentiated from direct services to individuals. The simplest way seemed to be to take payments by business firms to government as measuring intermediate services by the latter, thereby including in the calculation of national income (at the payments level) net business profits after all taxes. Likewise, direct payments by individuals to government were taken to measure final services, i.e., services by government to individuals as ultimate consumers. This meant including in national income (again at the payments level) all payments to individuals, gross of direct taxes paid by them.

Differences between the prices paid by government for the goods it purchased and those paid by other sectors of the economy were not adjusted for, except in the case of war products in *National Product in Wartime*. This is in line with the failure to make similar adjustments for price differentials among other sectors of the economy (e.g., between pricing on farmers' and on urban industries' markets).

Finally, it was deemed consistent to treat government as if it were a business corporation, and allow for its net savings or losses. This is tantamount to measuring the total value of government services by the taxes paid for them, rather than at cost—a basis exactly parallel to that applied in valuing the total output of other industries in the economy.

These answers leave plenty of room for doubt and contention,[38] and as the character of government activity changes and its functional characteristics are better analyzed, a less arbitrary approach may become feasible. But the essential difficulty will remain, viz., governments (and related semipublic sectors) and the private business sectors (both firms and individuals) do not and cannot operate under the same rules, any more than do or can the business and what may roughly be called the family sectors. The difficulties in handling the latter are reduced by excluding it almost completely from national income; but national income includes both the private business and the public sectors. The fundamental difference in the principles on which these sectors operate means that some arbitrary decisions will always be called for in order to put the two together—

[38]For extensive and repeated discussion of these problems, see *Studies in Income and Wealth* by the Conference on Research in Income and Wealth, particularly Vol. One (1937, pp. 175-248); Two (1938, pp. 269-342); Three (1939, Preface); Six (1943, pp. 1-44). For modification of the assumption in war years see *National Product in Wartime*, Part I.

by applying the private market or public economy base to both, or by devising some common denominator.

Though the bearing of differential pricing upon international comparisons of national income is obvious, we cannot end without stressing it. Differences in price bases among the several sectors of a nation's economy reflect differences in institutional characteristics and principles of operation. Even an industrially advanced nation with a democratic social system cannot be described as virtually one free business market. If the family and its economic life is omitted, there is still the farm sector, the public utility, the government—each with its peculiarities. When we consider more than one national economy, differences in the relative importance of various sectors within each are perhaps most prominent. Failure to adjust for price differentials among the several sectors in each country means that international comparisons cannot be made properly unless it is assumed that the relative distribution of national income among these various sectors as well as the extent of the intra-national price differentials are similar. Obviously, such an assumption is not valid. Hence international comparisons of levels, composition, and even changes in national income cannot be sound until some advance has been made toward adjusting for price differentials within each country. The customary basis for international comparisons of national income, exchange rates or market prices for a few commodities, is obviously so crude that only the biggest differences can be deemed significant.

5 Directions of Future Work

We have discussed some problems in the definition and interpretation of national income and of related totals, merely noted others, and not even mentioned quite a few (e.g., in measuring *national* income what constitutes a 'nation'; types of allocation, such as by industrial source). The reader may well be disturbed by the contrast between the quantitative definiteness of the estimates in Parts I-III and the challengeable character of the assumptions upon which they rest. Our critique of the bases of estimates may easily create the impression that they are shifting sand, and that the edifice built on them, with its impressive structure of quantitative precision, is unsound, a precarious indicator of the net contribution of the economy; indeed, that while judicious and cautious use of the estimates might serve a purpose, their appearance of finality and accuracy is likely to offset this service, so that it would be better to abstain altogether from such assessments, or at least to restrict them to academic cloisters.

Such counsel of despair is hardly warranted. First, we have harped upon the thorny problems and moot questions in national income definition and interpretation to the neglect of the wide sectors and many aspects that can be defined simply, measured properly, and interpreted easily. Second, agreement on certain basic assumptions, e.g., that concerning goals of economic activity and the corresponding distinction between gross and net, and the limitation of economic activity to narrower boundaries than all activities leading to the satisfaction of individuals' wants is widespread. Alternatives were discussed in order to ensure awareness of the character of the underlying assumptions and to caution the reader not to stretch the estimates beyond their bases. Third, if these assumptions concerning goals and the distinction between economic activity proper and life in general are accepted, the remaining questions are often of minor quantitative import. Except in years of violent changes and shifts (such, for example, as those of a major war) temporal changes in price can be tolerably well adjusted for; price differentials do not shift violently from year to year; the share of government and other nonfree market sectors is small, no matter how measured; illegal activities and transfers can easily be excluded, and the boundaries of a nation as an economic entity set. Of the remaining problems, some are theoretically not soluble, but even highly arbitrary solutions can have no more than a minor quantitative effect on the national income totals and their distributions.

At any rate the choice is not between retaining national income estimates and discarding them; and it is not even between not having and having widespread public discussion of these and related estimates. Society has always needed and searched for a commonly agreed upon yardstick by which to measure the success of its economic activity; the demand for such a yardstick became more intense as economic success was given a high place in the scale of social values, and sharp fluctuations occurred in economic activity. National income has not always been that yardstick. In this country before 1900, national wealth estimates were more numerous than national income— possibly reflecting the race to accumulate capital and attain an adequate level of industrial capacity. But in recent decades national income, with its emphasis on current contribution to both consumers and capital accumulation, has been used increasingly as the most convenient measure of economic progress, of even short term fluctuations. The more the estimates are so used, the greater the likelihood that they will be widely discussed—and properly so since their significance for public policy lies in widespread agreement concerning their underlying assumptions and their suitability as criteria of economic achievement. In an authoritarian regime national income could be made taboo as a subject of public discussion and the concept declared illegal or defined by dictatorial fiat. Its free acceptance in a democratic society gives it meaning as an appraisal based upon widely accepted criteria tested by discussion.

The choice is then between (a) letting national income estimates be taken at their face value and misinterpreted because of incomplete awareness of the underlying assumptions and (b) attempting to have them used and discussed in terms of their relevance to this or that specific problem or issue of public policy in full cognizance of the assumptions upon which the concept rests and the compromises in measurement forced by lack of data. There is no question of discarding them because they may be misused. The alternative is between trying and not trying to ensure their intelligent use. Critical probing of the basic assumptions and exposition of the limitations of the estimates, despite the acute intellectual discomfort entailed, serves both to encourage the valid use of the estimates and to indicate the directions of further investigation.

So far, national income measurement has been most successful in recording the contribution of the business area, least in the public and family sectors. Future study lies largely in the latter—both within a single economy and for several—because international comparisons cannot mean much unless the relative weight and relations of the three sectors in each economy are known.

The public sector especially should be analyzed more carefully and in greater detail. Government activities must be classified functionally, the comparative pricing of factors or products in government and private spheres reviewed, government current and capital expenditures differentiated. Taking total government expenditures on goods gross, as the Department of Commerce does, is useful for some immediate purposes but does not solve the cardinal problem of measuring the government's share in the *net* product of economic activity. Study of the different types of relation between the government and private spheres in different economies will reveal major problems and facilitate the development of common bases upon which activities in the private and the public sectors can be consistently measured, compared, and combined.

The family sector also should be studied more thoroughly. The interest in recent years in the size distribution of income among individuals and households and in consumers' expenditures is a step toward linking the family and business sectors. As these studies of size distributions and of consumption-savings patterns progress, it will become increasingly possible to take account of household nonmarket activities of an economic character; to extend national income estimates over more of these nonmarket activities; and to adjust dollar totals for price differentials among various groups of consumers. Again, as other countries are covered, the ground will be laid for comparative studies of economic growth and change in national economies differing in social organization.

The more intensive analysis of the government and family sectors will not only add to the reliability of estimates for some components of national income; it will also permit types of allocation not feasible at present. But we should not overlook the other tasks that remain within the framework of the national income estimates as they are currently prepared. The reconciliation of the estimates made by the flow of payments and the final product approaches, both with respect to the over-all totals and the apportionment between consumption and saving, is one. The extension of measurements to various gross product totals, to a point of approximating the total volume of transactions is another. The translation of estimates for different countries to as comparable a set of bases as is possible with the present data is a third. And there are always the tasks of continually refining the measures, and establishing them for finer classifications and more frequent time intervals.

Much progress will undoubtedly be made in all these directions within the next twenty-five years. Moreover, the estimates will prove more revealing and useful simply because of the mere cumulation of data and experience. Yet we cannot hope ever to resolve fully the conceptual and statistical problems. At any time, conceptual problems in national income measurement are colored by conflicts concerning the purposes of economic activity, the relative importance of various sectors of the economy, and of economic and other useful activities. Unless such conflicts cease, either by suppression or by some improbable stabilization of economic and social life in fixed channels, definitions of national income and its components will reflect compromises made in the interest of consistent and continuous measurement. And such compromises will always be subject to critical scrutiny and to challenge as less good than others for specific uses. Likewise, statistical problems arising from lack of data will continue to hamper the estimator until society becomes more cognizant of the need and takes the initiative in seeing that they are gathered currently. Because of the huge cost of collecting nationwide data, they have been gathered in the past (usually by the government) only when society became convinced that the problems for whose solution they seemed essential were crucial. Consequently the accumulation of data has lagged behind the emergence of problems calling for quantitative analysis. The statistical expedients that will continue to be resorted to and the consequent approximations will give rise, as they should, to different procedures and judgments concerning the reliability of the several estimates. Some sectors it would be desirable to measure will still be omitted because no procedure for reaching even satisfactory approximations can be devised.

Like all social measurement, national income estimates will never be beyond criticism on the score of reliability or completeness of coverage, or beyond dispute as to the validity of underlying assumptions. But this, of course, is no reason for not using them now, or for not continuing work on their extension and improvement in the future. Despite all their imperfections, the estimates are indispensable for taking a broad view of the economy; and for testing in the light of a record of the past and the immediate present the ever changing theories of economic behavior, diagnoses of economic problems, and pleas for economic reform. It is not unreasonably sanguine to hope that continuation, extension, and refinement of these estimates will assure an even greater contribution to a better understanding of economic life and to a more intelligent handling of the various problems that find their roots in the workings of the economy.

INDEX

Relation of the Directors to the Work and Publications
of the
National Bureau of Economic Research

1. The object of the National Bureau of Economic Research is to ascertain and to present to the public important economic facts and their interpretation in a scientific and impartial manner. The Board of Directors is charged with the responsibility of ensuring that the work of the Bureau is carried on in strict conformity with this object.

2. To this end the Board of Directors shall appoint one or more Directors of Research.

3. The Director or Directors of Research shall submit to the members of the Board, or to its Executive Committee, for their formal adoption, all specific proposals concerning researches to be instituted.

4. No report shall be published until the Director or Directors of Research shall have submitted to the Board a summary drawing attention to the character of the data and their utilization in the report, the nature and treatment of the problems involved, the main conclusions and such other information as in their opinion would serve to determine the suitability of the report for publication in accordance with the principles of the Bureau.

5. A copy of any manuscript proposed for publication shall also be submitted to each member of the Board. For each manuscript to be so submitted a special committee shall be appointed by the President, or at his designation by the Executive Director, consisting of three Directors selected as nearly as may be one from each general division of the Board. The names of the special manuscript committee shall be stated to each Director when the summary and report described in paragraph (4) are sent to him. It shall be the duty of each member of the committee to read the manuscript. If each member of the special committee signifies his approval within thirty days, the manuscript may be published. If each member of the special committee has not signified his approval within thirty days of the transmittal of the report and manuscript, the Director of Research shall then notify each member of the Board, requesting approval or disapproval of publication, and thirty additional days shall be granted for this purpose. The manuscript shall then not be published unless at least a majority of the entire Board and a two-thirds majority of those members of the Board who shall have voted on the proposal within the time fixed for the receipt of votes on the publication proposed shall have approved.

6. No manuscript may be published, though approved by each member of the special committee, until forty-five days have elapsed from the transmittal of the summary and report. The interval is allowed for the receipt of any memorandum of dissent or reservation, together with a brief statement of his reasons, that any member may wish to express; and such memorandum of dissent or reservation shall be published with the manuscript if he so desires. Publication does not, however, imply that each member of the Board has read the manuscript, or that either members of the Board in general, or of the special committee, have passed upon its validity in every detail.

7. A copy of this resolution shall, unless otherwise determined by the Board, be printed in each copy of every National Bureau book.

(Resolution adopted October 25, 1926 and revised February 6, 1933 and February 24, 1941)

NATIONAL BUREAU OF ECONOMIC RESEARCH PUBLICATIONS IN REPRINT

An Arno Press Series

Barger, Harold. **The Transportation Industries, 1889-1946:**
A Study of Output, Employment, and Productivity. 1951

Barger, Harold and Hans H. Landsberg. **American Agriculture,**
1899-1939: A Study of Output, Employment, and Productivity.
1942

Barger, Harold and Sam H. Schurr. **The Mining Industries,**
1899-1939: A Study of Output, Employment, and Productivity.
1944

Burns, Arthur F. **The Frontiers of Economic Knowledge.** 1954

Committee of the President's Conference on Unemployment.
Business Cycles and Unemployment. 1923

Conference of the Universities-National Bureau Committee for
Economic Research. **Aspects of Labor Economics.** 1962

Conference of the Universities-National Bureau Committee for
Economic Research. **Business Concentration and Price**
Policy. 1955

Conference of the Universities-National Bureau Committee for
Economic Research. **Capital Formation and Economic**
Growth. 1955

Conference of the Universities-National Bureau Committee for
Economic Research. **Policies to Combat Depression.** 1956

Conference of the Universities-National Bureau Committee for
Economic Research. **The State of Monetary Economics.**
[1963]

Conference of the Universities-National Bureau Committee for
Economic Research and the Committee on Economic Growth of
the Social Science Research Council. **The Rate and Direction**
of Inventive Activity: Economic and Social Factors. 1962

Conference on Research in Income and Wealth. **Input-Output**
Analysis: An Appraisal. 1955

Conference on Research in Income and Wealth. **Problems of**
Capital Formation: Concepts, Measurement, and Controlling
Factors. 1957

Conference on Research in Income and Wealth. **Trends in the**
American Economy in the Nineteenth Century. 1960

Conference on Research in National Income and Wealth.
Studies in Income and Wealth. 1937

Copeland, Morris A. **Trends in Government Financing.** 1961

Fabricant, Solomon. **Employment in Manufacturing, 1899-1939:**
An Analysis of Its Relation to the Volume of Production. 1942

Fabricant, Solomon. **The Output of Manufacturing Industries,**
1899-1937. 1940

Goldsmith, Raymond W.   **Financial Intermediaries in the American Economy Since 1900.** 1958

Goldsmith, Raymond W.   **The National Wealth of the United States in the Postwar Period.** 1962

Kendrick, John W.   **Productivity Trends in the United States.** 1961

Kuznets, Simon.   **Capital in the American Economy:** Its Formation and Financing. 1961

Kuznets, Simon.   **Commodity Flow and Capital Formation.** Vol. One. 1938

Kuznets, Simon.   **National Income:** A Summary of Findings. 1946

Kuznets, Simon.   **National Income and Capital Formation, 1919-1935:** A Preliminary Report. 1937

Kuznets, Simon.   **National Product in Wartime.** 1945

Kuznets, Simon.   **National Product Since 1869.** 1946

Kuznets, Simon.   **Seasonal Variations in Industry and Trade.** 1933

Long, Clarence D.   **Wages and Earnings in the United States, 1860-1890.** 1960

Mendershausen, Horst.   **Changes in Income Distribution During the Great Depression.** 1946

Mills, Frederick C.   **Economic Tendencies in the United States:** Aspects of Pre-War and Post-War Changes. 1932

Mills, Frederick C.   **Price-Quantity Interactions in Business Cycles.** 1946

Mills, Frederick C.   **The Behavior of Prices.** 1927

Mitchell, Wesley C.   **Business Cycles:** The Problem and Its Setting. [1927]

Mitchell, Wesley C., et al.   **Income in the United States:** Its Amount and Distribution 1909-1919. Volume One, Summary. [1921]

Mitchell, Wesley C., editor.   **Income in the United States:** Its Amount and Distribution 1909-1919. Volume Two, Detailed Report. 1922

National Accounts Review Committee of the National Bureau of Economic Research.   **The National Economic Accounts of the United States.** 1958

Rees, Albert.   **Real Wages in Manufacturing, 1890-1914.** 1961

Stigler, George J.   **Capital and Rates of Return in Manufacturing Industries.** 1963

Wealth Inventory Planning Study, The George Washington University.   **Measuring the Nation's Wealth.** 1964

Williams, Pierce.   **The Purchase of Medical Care Through Fixed Periodic Payment.** 1932

Wolman, Leo.   **The Growth of American Trade Unions, 1880-1923.** 1924

Woolley, Herbert B.   **Measuring Transactions Between World Areas.** 1966

DATE DUE